Praise for *The Gardens of Democracy*

"*The Gardens of Democracy* provides a refreshing new conceptual approach to understanding our economic and political situation, and it will help us move past the fossilized ideas in today's public debates."

FRANCIS FUKUYAMA, *author of* The Origins of Political Order *and Olivier Nomellini Senior Fellow, Freeman Spogli Institute for International Studies, Stanford University*

"In highly engaging style, Liu and Hanauer capture the revolution underway in our understanding of how economies and social systems work. They offer a provocative, inspiring vision of citizenship, democracy, and the role of government. This slender book with big ambitions deserves to be read, debated, and read again."

ERIC BEINHOCKER, *author of* The Origin of Wealth

"Society is a garden. Liu and Hanauer's simple metaphor makes the complexities and limits of social policy emerge before your eyes. Statists can't see the interconnections of organic systems. Free marketers can't see that a garden needs some tending. If you're looking for a way forward out of America's dangerous gridlock, read this wonderful book."

JONATHAN HAIDT, *professor of psychology, University of Virginia, and author of* The Righteous Mind: Why Good People are Divided by Politics and Religion

"Eric Liu and Nick Hanauer are progressives who always think outside the box, and that's why everyone should pay attention to them. *The Gardens of Democracy* shakes up our stale debate over government's role in a dynamic society, and in a thoughtful, creative, and inventive way. Everyone will find something to disagree with here, and that's the point: getting us out of our comfort zones is an immensely useful democratic undertaking."

E. J. DIONNE JR., *author of* Why Americans Hate Politics

"Liu and Hanauer get it right. They powerfully show how the complex, modern world requires new thinking and new policies that recognize the adaptive, mutualist nature of our economic, political, and social systems. This is a fabulous book!"

SCOTT E. PAGE, *author of* Diversity and Complexity *and director of the Center for the Study of Complex Systems, University of Michigan*

"The great contribution of Eric Liu and Nick Hanauer in *The Gardens of Democracy* is to explain how the very categories we use to think about our political problems prevent us from understanding and solving them. They're a scouting party venturing upriver for the rest of us, and we'd be foolish not to heed their reports."

MICHAEL TOMASKY, *editor,* Democracy: A Journal of Ideas

THE Gardens *of* Democracy

THE
Gardens
of Democracy

*A New American Story of
Citizenship, the Economy, and
the Role of Government*

ERIC LIU AND NICK HANAUER

SASQUATCH BOOKS
SEATTLE

Printed in the United States of America
Published by Sasquatch Books
17 16 15 14 13 12   9 8 7 6 5 4 3 2

Book design by View Design Company
Cover illustration by Steven Noble
Interior illustrations by James Provost

Library of Congress Cataloging-in-Publication Data is available.
ISBN-13: 978-1-57061-823-9
ISBN-10: 1-57061-823-2

Sasquatch Books
119 South Main Street, Suite 400
Seattle, WA 98104
(206) 467-4300
www.sasquatchbooks.com
custserv@sasquatchbooks.com

For more information, please visit www.godemocracy.net.

CONTENTS

Of Gardens and Gardeners

Effective gardening requires the right setting: fertile soil, good light, water.

It requires a strong view as to what should and should not be grown.

It requires a loving willingness to tend constantly, to fertilize and nurture what we seed.

It requires a hard-headed willingness to weed what does not belong.

Great gardeners would never simply "let nature take its course." They take responsibility for their gardens.

Great gardeners assume change in weather and circumstance. They adapt.

Great gardens are sustainable only with continuous investment and renewal. Great gardeners turn the soil and rotate the plantings.

Human beings, it is said, originated in a garden. Perhaps this is why all of us understand so intuitively what it takes to be great gardeners.

I. Seeds

Gardenbrain vs. Machinebrain

*The failure of our politics to keep pace with reality—
The way ideology prevents adaption—New science
gives us new sight about how the world works—What
must follow is a new story: about self-interest, the meaning
of citizenship, the nature of the economy, and the role
of government—The gardens of democracy*

AMERICA IS AN EXPERIMENT. It is an experiment in democracy, still the greatest the world has ever seen. But it is also, like every nation, human community, or living organism, an experiment in evolution.

One thing that has made America exceptional thus far has been its ability to adapt. From the founding onward, this nation has reckoned with its own internal contradictions and with external threats—the insufficiency of the Articles of Confederation, the poison pill of slavery, the rise of the Robber Barons, the emergence of totalitarian enemies—and it has evolved successfully in response to such circumstances.

The question today is, can we still adapt? Will our experiment get another cycle? Or has our society's capacity to evolve run its course?

The failure of American politics to address and solve the great challenges of our time—climate change, debt and deficits, worsening schools, rising health care costs, the shriveling of the middle class—is not just a failure of will or nerve. It is equally a failure of ideas and understanding. And the failure to address these challenges isn't just a matter of politics, but of survival.

To begin with, we labor today under a painfully confining choice between outmoded ideologies on both the left and the right. On the left, too many remain wedded to paradigms first formed during the decades between the Progressive Era and the New Deal. They are top-down, prescriptive, bureaucratic notions about how to address social challenges. These state-centric approaches made sense in a centralizing, industrializing America. They make much less sense in the networked economy and polity of today.

On the right, we hear ideas even more historically irrelevant: laissez-faire economics and a "don't tread on me" idea of citizenship that might have been tolerable in 1775 when the country had 3 million largely agrarian inhabitants, only some of whom could vote, but is at best naïve and at worst destructive in a diverse, interdependent, largely urban nation of over 300 million.

Our politics has become an over-rehearsed, over-ritualized piece of stage combat between these two old ideologies. False choice after polarizing false choice emanates from Washington. Both ideologies—indeed, the surrender of American politics to ideology itself, and the abandonment of pragmatism as a guiding political philosophy—

make it harder by the day for America to adapt.

We wrote this short book to offer a new way. We aim to reach not "moderates" or "centrists" who split the difference between left and right. We aim to reach those who think independently. That might mean those who claim no party affiliation, though it also includes many loyal Democrats and Republicans. It definitely means those who are uncomfortable being confined by narrow choices, old paradigms, and zero-sum outcomes.

If you can hold these paired thoughts in your head, we wrote this book for you:

- –The federal government spends too much money. The wealthy should pay much more in taxes.

- –Every American should have access to high-quality health care. We spend far too much on health care in the United States already.

- –We need to eliminate our dependence on fossil fuels. We need to ensure our economy continues to grow.

- –Unions are a crucially important part of our economy and society. Unions have become overly protectionist and are in need of enormous amounts of reform.

- –We need strong government. We need strong citizens.

Contemporary American political discourse sees these pairings as *either-or*. Independent-thinking Americans see them as *both-and*. Our goal in these pages is to push past the one-dimensional, left-right choices of contemporary politics—between more government or less, selfishness and altruism, suffocating collectivism and market fundamentalism—and find *orthogonal* approaches to our challenges. The great challenge of this age—and the point of this book—is to rethink how we as citizens create change, how the economy truly works, and what government fundamentally is *for*. The great challenge of this age is to change how we *see*, and by so doing, improve our ability to adapt.

At every stage in history, people operate within a constructed frame of ideas, metaphors, and narratives—and this story frame defines how people think of themselves, what they think is possible in life, and how they think the world works. To put it more pointedly, there is not now and has never been some abstracted social reality "out there"; at every moment in each epoch, in ways influenced by culture, science, and technology, people *construct* a social reality that validates some truths and distorts others. These frames define what we think of as good for us—how we pursue our individual and collective self-interest. It defines what a society thinks is possible.

But these frames are not fixed. Every so often, the idea set shifts radically, and with it our notion of what is good for us. We are in the midst of such a shift right now. A set of quiet scientific revolutions now demands that we see in terms of systems—and enables us to make sense of them. What kinds of *systems* make up our economy, our society, and the ecologies that sustain us? How are the elements in these systems *connected*? And finally, how do the agents (people) within these systems *behave*?

These are the kinds of questions we are far better able to answer today than we were half a century ago. Science—which we mean broadly to include physical discoveries, insights into behavior, awareness of patterns of experience—tells us today that the world is a *complex adaptive system*, not a linear equilibrium system; that the elements within it are *networked*, not atomized; that humans operate in that system as *emotional reciprocal approximators*, not rational self-regarding calculators.

Taken together, these insights (which we describe in more depth below) suggest a new narrative about how strong societies emerge, adapt, and thrive.

Why does this matter? Why should anyone besides students of science or intellectual history care? Because in every age, those who define the metaphors define the terms of politics. In its time, Darwin's theory of evolution was corrupted into a powerful ideology of Social Darwinism, which treated the weak and marginalized as presumptively unfit for survival (and government aid). Later, Taylorism and "scientific management" led government leaders to believe they could engineer their way to desired social outcomes. In our own time, the belief that markets follow the equilibrium dynamics of physics has had its own awful results. Consider that policymakers did not foresee or forestall the crash of 2008 because their dominant economic model had, as Alan Greenspan later admitted, "a flaw"— namely, that it didn't contemplate human irrationality.

This is not just about economics or politics; it's about *imagination* and our ability to conceive of new ways of conceiving of things. It is about our ability to adapt and evolve in the face of changing circumstances and the consequences of our actions. History shows that civilizations tend eventually to get stuck in the patterns that had brought them success. They can either stay stuck and decay, or get unstuck and thrive.

We posit in these pages that this country has for too long been stuck in a mode of seeing and thinking called Machinebrain. We argue that the time has come for a new mode of public imagination that we call Gardenbrain.

Machinebrain sees the world and democracy as a series of mechanisms—clocks and gears, perpetual motion machines, balances and counterbalances. Machinebrain requires you to conceive of the economy as perfectly efficient and automatically self-correcting. Machinebrain presupposes stability and predictability, and only grudgingly admits the need for correction. Even the word commonly used for such correction—"regulation"—is mechanical in origin and regrettable in connotation.

Gardenbrain sees the world and democracy as an entwined set of ecosystems—sinks and sources of trust and social capital, webs of economic growth, networks of behavioral contagion. Gardenbrain forces you to conceive of the economy as man-made and effective only if well constructed and well cared-for. Gardenbrain presupposes instability and unpredictability, and thus expects a continuous need for seeding, feeding, and weeding everchanging systems. To be a gardener is not to let nature take its course; it is to *tend*. It is to accept responsibility for nurturing the good growth and killing the bad. *Tending* and *regulating* thus signify the same work, but tending frames the work as presumptively necessary and beneficial rather than as something to be suffered.

Machinebrain treats people as cogs: votes to be collected by political machines; consumers to be manipulated by marketing machines; employees to be plugged into industrial machines. It is a static mindset of control and fixity, and is the basis of most of our inherited institutions, from schools to corporations to prisons.

Gardenbrain sees people as interdependent creators of a dynamic world: our emotions affect each other; our personal choices cascade into public patterns, which can be shaped but rarely controlled. It is a dynamic mindset of influence and evolution, of direction without control, and is the basis of our future.

Machinebrain allows you to rationalize atomized selfishness and a neglect of larger problems. It accepts social ills like poverty, environmental degradation, and ignorance as the inevitable outcome of an efficient marketplace. It is fatalistic and reductionist, treating change as an unnecessary and risky deviation from the norm.

Gardenbrain recognizes such social ills and the shape of our society as the byproduct of man-made arrangements. It is evolutionary and holistic, treating change as the norm, essential and full of opportunity. It leads you to acknowledge that human societies thrive only through active gardening.

Gardenbrain changes everything.

New understandings about how the world works—and the development of tools to represent such understandings—now undermine the ideologies of hyperindividualism on the right and reflexive statism on the left. Science is coming ever closer to depicting what each of us already understands intuitively about how the world works. Most of us know in our gut—contrary to the political ethos of raw self-seeking—that our family, friends, neighbors, and customers are bound by something other than raw calculation of interest. We know in our gut—contrary to the axioms of market fundamentalism—that businesses and

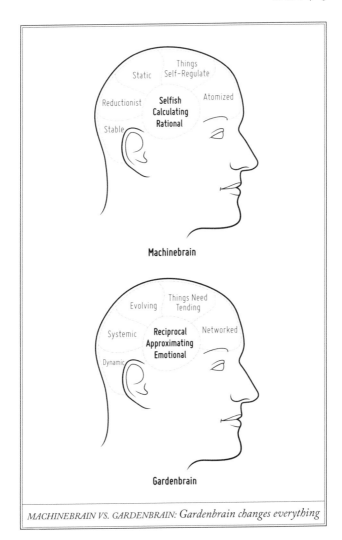

Machinebrain

Gardenbrain

MACHINEBRAIN VS. GARDENBRAIN: Gardenbrain changes everything

economies are not self-regulating machines. We know in our gut as well—contrary to the promises of expert-led government—that a society that relies on top-down problem-solving ends up being too slow and too non-adaptive to thrive.

So now for the plan of this book.

We will begin by summarizing the revolutions in human understanding that have fundamentally altered our mac-rocosmic understanding of societies. We will explore in detail how these new ideas—ideas about people and the systems in which they operate—transform how we think about our self-interest and the public interest. Our claim here is that new ways of understanding the world trans-late into profoundly new ways of thinking about how to advance our shared interests—and that our politics must change to reflect that.

In our first book, *The True Patriot*, we argued that putting self above community and country was morally wrong. In this book, we argue that it is stupid. We aim to show that in theory and in practice, self-seeking is now a counter-productive instinct and that we need a bigger idea of what freedom means in order for our country to remain great.

Next we unpack how these ideas and metaphors impact what we think of as the three "gardens of democracy," the interlocking organic realms that comprise public life: citi-zenship, economy, and government.

We will argue that understanding the world in these new ways raises the standard for citizenship, by making clearer the ways in which our individual behavior inescapably creates feedback loops that contagiously shape society. Our new understanding of citizenship forces us to acknowledge that we are individually both more powerful within, and more responsible to, the communities and networks that surround us.

Then we will explore how understanding the economy as a complex adaptive system fundamentally challenges and changes our notions of what wealth is, how it is generated, and why fairness and fierce competition are allies. Powerful new metaphors with explanatory power will lead us to new and surprising conclusions about how we should organize our economy. We'll make an argument for a "true capitalism" both more competitive and more fair than what we now call capitalism.

Finally, we will explore the question of what government is for and how it should be constructed, given our new understanding of social systems and the world around us. Our aim is to pose the deepest questions about the role of government in modern democratic society and go all the way back to first principles in constructing its proper role. Government is not, as both today's liberals and conservatives seem to think, a thing "over there" to be lionized or reviled. In this section, we aim to reboot a conversation on the actual civic meaning of self-government, beyond acting out or opting out, beyond spectator sport or simple cynicism. How does a diverse, networked, interdependent, largely urban and technological society govern itself?

We acknowledge that we could have written separate books on these three topics: citizenship, economy, role of government. But our aim was precisely to show that these things are connected—not least by a need for new thinking and new seeing. In making our book short, we know that we trade detail for perspective. We simply believe this is a time when perspective matters most.

Thus we close the book by trying to put into historical context the need for America now to grow up—and the need for us to understand freedom not only as personal liberty but also as the collective force that fuels adaption and survival. Our extraordinary experiment in democracy and capitalism is over 230 years old. We Americans are not children anymore. Indeed, some think that the nation is in rapid decline. We completely disagree. We think of America as an adolescent or young adult coming into our prime, full of promise, energy, and enthusiasm for the challenges of our times—but in need of maturation of thought, habit, and awareness. The words enshrined in the Jefferson Memorial, written 40 years after the Declaration and 43 years before Darwin authored *Origin of Species*, capture this spirit perfectly:

I am not an advocate for frequent changes in laws and constitutions. But laws and institutions must go hand in hand with the progress of the human mind. As that becomes more developed, more enlightened, as new discoveries are made, new truths discovered and manners and opinions change, with the change of circumstances, institutions must advance also to keep pace with the times. We might as well require a man to wear still the coat which fitted him when a boy as civilized society to remain ever under the regimen of their barbarous ancestors.

In *The True Patriot*, we challenged our readers to define for themselves what their moral code was, even if they rejected the one we put forth. Our argument was that having a code always beats not having one. We now make a similar appeal. You may find our metaphors and arguments about the gardens of our democracy to be wrong-headed or unsatisfying. But any serious and honest reader must admit the need to reimagine how we do democracy. So if you don't like our frame, we invite you to put forth your own. Offer up an alternative. Experiment. It's the American way. It's the only way now for America to evolve.

II. Self-Interest

True Self-Interest Is Mutual Interest

*Self-interest may be a basic human condition and
a constant in politics, but how we conceptualize self-interest
has, at key moments in history, changed fundamentally—
The Enlightenment was one such moment; the science
of our current age is giving us another—We compare
and contrast these old and new stories of systems, causation,
and agency—The fundamental shift of this second
Enlightenment is from atomized individualism
to networked interdependence, and this forces a
new concept of self-interest*

What Is Self-Interest?

POLITICS IN A DEMOCRACY can be understood many ways, but on one level it is the expression of where people believe their self-interest lies—that is to say, "what is good for me?" Even when voters vote according to primal affinities or fears rather than economic advantage (as Thomas Frank, in *What's the Matter With Kansas?*, lamented of poor whites who vote Republican), it is because they've come to define self-interest more in terms of those primal identities than in terms of dollars and cents.

This is not proof of the stupidity of such voters. It is proof of the malleability and multidimensionality of self-interest. While *the degree to which* human beings pursue that which they think is good for them has not and will probably never change, *what they believe is good for them* can change and from time to time has, radically.

In the pages to come, we assert a simple proposition: that fundamental shifts in popular understanding of how the world works *necessarily produce* fundamental shifts in our conception of self-interest, which in turn *necessarily produce* fundamental shifts in how we think to order our societies.

Consider for a moment this simple example:

For the overwhelming majority of human history, people looked up into the sky and saw the sun, moon, stars, and planets revolve around the earth. This bedrock assumption based on everyday observation framed our self-conception as a species and our interpretation of everything around us.

Alas, it was completely wrong.

Advances in both observation technology and scientific understanding allowed people to first *see*, and much later *accept*, that in fact the earth was not the center of the universe, but rather, a speck in an ever-enlarging and increasingly humbling and complex cosmos. We are not the center of the universe.

It's worth reflecting for a moment on the fact that the evidence for this scientific truth was there the whole time. But people didn't perceive it until concepts like gravity allowed us to imagine the possibility of orbits. New understanding turns simple observation into meaningful perception. Without it, what one observes can be radically misinterpreted. New understanding can completely change the way we see a situation and how we see our self-interest with respect to it. Concepts determine, and often distort, percepts.

Today, most of the public is unaware that we are in the

midst of a moment of new understanding. In recent decades, a revolution has taken place in our scientific and mathematical understanding of the systemic nature of the world we inhabit.

–We used to understand the world as stable and predictable, and now we see that it is unstable and inherently impossible to predict.

–We used to assume that what you do in one place has little or no effect on what happens in another place, but now we understand that small differences in initial choices can cascade into huge variations in ultimate consequences.

–We used to assume that people are primarily rational, and now we see that they are primarily emotional.

Now, consider: how might these new shifts in understanding affect our sense of who we are and what is good for us?

A Second Enlightenment and the Radical Redefinition of Self-Interest

In traditional economic theory, as in politics, we Americans are taught to believe that selfishness is next to godliness. We are taught that the market is at its most efficient when individuals act rationally to maximize their own self-interest without regard to the effects on anyone

else. We are taught that democracy is at its most functional when individuals and factions pursue their own
self-interest aggressively. In both instances, we are taught
that an invisible hand converts this relentless clash and
competition of self-seekers into a greater good.

These teachings are half right: most people indeed are looking out for themselves. We have no illusions about that.
But the teachings are half wrong in that they enshrine a
particular, and particularly narrow, notion of what it means
to look out for oneself.

Conventional wisdom conflates self-interest and selfishness. It makes sense to be self-interested in the long run.
It does not make sense to be reflexively selfish in every
transaction. And that, unfortunately, is what market fundamentalism and libertarian politics promote: a brand of
selfishness that is profoundly against our actual interest.

Let's back up a step.

When Thomas Jefferson wrote in the Declaration of Independence that certain truths were held to be "self-evident,"
he was not recording a timeless fact; he was asserting one
into being. Today we read his words through the filter
of modernity. We assume that those truths had always
been self-evident. But they weren't. They most certainly
were not a generation before Jefferson wrote. In the quar-
ter century between 1750 and 1775, in a confluence of

dramatic changes in science, politics, religion, and economics, a group of enlightened British colonists in America grew gradually more open to the idea that all men are created equal and are endowed by their Creator with certain unalienable rights.

It took Jefferson's assertion, and the Revolution that followed, to *make* those truths self-evident.

We point this out as a simple reminder. Every so often in history, new truths about human nature and the nature of human societies crystallize. Such paradigmatic shifts build gradually but cascade suddenly.

This has certainly been the case with prevailing ideas about what constitutes self-interest. Self-interest, it turns out, is not a fixed entity that can be objectively defined and held constant. It is a malleable, culturally embodied notion.

Think about it. Before the Enlightenment, the average serf believed that his destiny was foreordained. He fatalistically understood the scope of life's possibility to be circumscribed by his status at birth. His concept of self-interest extended only as far as that of his nobleman. His station was fixed, and reinforced by tradition and social ritual. His hopes for betterment were pinned on the afterlife. Post-Enlightenment, that all changed. The average European now believed he was master of his own destiny. Instead of worrying about his odds of a good afterlife, he worried about improving his lot here and now. He was motivated to advance beyond what had seemed fated. He was inclined to be skeptical about received notions of what was possible in life.

The multiple revolutions of the Enlightenment—scientific, philosophical, spiritual, material, political—substituted reason for doctrine, agency for fatalism, independence for obedience, scientific method for superstition, human ambition for divine predestination. Driving this change was a new physics and mathematics that made the world seem rational and linear and subject to human mastery.

The science of that age had enormous explanatory and predictive power, and it yielded an entirely new way of conceptualizing self-interest. Now the individual, relying on his own wits, was to be celebrated for looking out for himself—and was expected to do so. As physics developed into a story of zero-sum collisions, as man mastered steam and made machines, as Darwin's theories of natural selection and evolution took hold, the binding and life-defining power of old traditions and institutions waned. A new belief seeped osmotically across disciplines and domains: Every man can make himself anew. And before long, this mutated into another ethic: Every man *for* himself.

Compared to the backward-looking, authority-worshipping, passive notion of self-interest that had previously prevailed, this, to be sure, was astounding progress. It was liberation. Nowhere more than in America—a land of wide-open spaces, small populations, and easily erased histories—did this atomized ideal of self-interest take hold. As Steven Watts describes in his groundbreaking history *The Republic Reborn*, "the cult of the self-made man" emerged in the first three decades after Independence. The civic ethos of the founding evaporated amidst the giddy free-agent opportunity to stake a claim and enrich oneself. Two centuries later, our greed-celebrating, ambition-soaked culture still echoes this original song of self-interest and individualism.

Over time, the rational self-seeking of the American has been elevated into an ideology now as strong and total-izing as the divine right of kings once was in medieval Europe. *Homo economicus*, the rationalist self-seeker of orthodox economics, along with his cousin *Homo politi-cus*, gradually came to define what is considered normal in the market and politics. We've convinced ourselves that a million individual acts of selfishness magically add up to a common good. And we've paid a great price for such arrogance. We have today a dominant legal and economic doctrine that treats people as disconnected automatons and treats the mess we leave behind as someone else's problem. We also have, in the Great Recession, painful evidence of the limits of this doctrine's usefulness.

But now a new story is unfolding.

Our century is yielding a second Enlightenment, and the narrative it offers about what makes us tick, individually and collectively, is infinitely more sophisticated than what we got the last time around. Since the mid-1960s, there have been profound advances in how we understand the systemic nature of botany, biology, physics, computer science, neuroscience, oceanography, atmospheric science, cognitive science, zoology, psychology, epidemiology, and even, yes, economics. Across these fields, a set of conceptual shifts is underway:

> Simple → Complex
>
> Atomistic → Networked
>
> Equilibrium → Disequilibrium
>
> Linear → Non-linear
>
> Mechanistic → Behavioral
>
> Efficient → Effective
>
> Predictive → Adaptive
>
> Independent → Interdependent
>
> Individual ability → Group diversity
>
> Rational calculator → Irrational approximators
>
> Selfish → Strongly reciprocal
>
> Win-lose → Win-win or lose-lose
>
> Competition → Cooperation

These shifts, of course, are not as clean or simple as they may appear in such a list. We acknowledge that there are volumes of nuance condensed here. But at a macro level, these shifts are real, consequential, and too often unseen.

Simple → Complex

The reductionist spirit of the first Enlightenment yielded a passion for classification—of species, of races, of types of all kinds of things—and this had the virtue of clarifying and simplifying what had once seemed fuzzy. But Enlightenment mathematics was limited in its ability to depict complicated systems like ecosystems and economies. The second Enlightenment is giving us the tools to understand complexity, as Scott Page and John Miller explain in *Complex Adaptive Systems*. Such systems—whether they are stock markets or immune systems, biospheres or political movements—are made of interacting agents, operating interdependently and unpredictably, learning from experience at individual and collective levels. The patterns we see are not mere aggregations of isolated acts but are the dynamic, emergent properties of all these interactions. The way these patterns behave may not be predictable, but they can be understood. We understand now how whirlpools arise from turbulence, or how bubbles emerge from economic activity.

Atomistic → Networked

The first Enlightenment was excellent for breaking phenomena into component parts, ever smaller and more
discrete. It was an atomic worldview that conceptualized
us as separate and independent. The second Enlightenment proves that while we are made of atoms we are *not*
atoms—that is, we behave not in atomistic ways but as
permeable, changeable parts of great networks and ecosystems. In particular, human societies are made up of vast,
many-to-many networks that have far greater impact on
us as individuals and on the shape and nature of our communities than we ever realized. The "six degrees" phenomenon is not a party game; it is a way of seeing more clearly
what Albert-Laszlo Barabasi, author of *Linked*, describes
as "scale-free networks": networks with an uneven distribution of connectedness, whose unevenness shapes
how people behave. Recognizing ourselves as part of
networks—rather than as isolated agents or even niches
in a hierarchy—enables us to see behavior as contagious,
even many degrees away. We are all on the network, part
of the same web, for better or worse. Thus does consumption of Middle East oil produce climate change, which
creates drought in North Africa, which raises food prices
there, which leads a vendor in Tunis to set himself afire,
which sparks a revolution that upends the Middle East.

Equilibrium → Disequilibrium

Classical economics, with us still today, relied upon 19th-century ideas from physics about systems in equilibrium. On this account, shocks or inputs to the system eventually result in the system going back to equilibrium, like water in a bucket or a ball bearing in a bowl (or the body returning to "stasis" after "sickness"). Such systems are closed, stable, and predictable. By contrast, complex systems like ecosystems and economies (or hurricanes or Facebook) are open and never stay in equilibrium. In non-equilibrium systems, a tiny input can create a catastrophic change—the so-called butterfly effect. The natural, emergent state of such systems—open rather than closed—is not stability but rather booms and busts, bubbles and crashes. It is from this tumult, says Eric Beinhocker, author of the magisterial *The Origin of Wealth*, that evolutionary opportunities for innovation and wealth creation arise.

Linear → Non-linear

The first Enlightenment emphasized linear, predictable models for change, whether at the atomic or the global level. The second Enlightenment emphasizes the butterfly effect, path dependence, high sensitivity to initial conditions and high volatility thereafter: in short, it gives us chaos, complexity, and non-linearity. What once seemed predictable is now understood to be quite unpredictable.

Mechanistic → Behavioral

The first Enlightenment made the stable, order-seeking machine the generative metaphor for economic activity (assembly lines), social organization (political machines), and government's role (that of a mechanic or clockmaker). The second Enlightenment studies not how people process things independently but rather how they behave interdependently. As David Brooks describes in *The Social Animal*, behavior is contagious, often unconsciously and unpredictably so, and individual choices can cascade suddenly into great waves of social change.

Efficient → Effective

The metaphors of the Enlightenment, taken to scale during the Industrial Age, led us to conceptualize markets as running with "machine-like efficiency" and frictionless alignment of supply and demand. But in fact, complex systems are tuned not for efficiency but for *effectiveness*—not for perfect solutions but for adaptive, resilient, *good-enough* solutions. This, as Rafe Sagarin depicts in the interdisciplinary survey *Natural Security*, is how nature works. It is how social and economic systems work too. Evolution relentlessly churns out effective, good-enough-for-now solutions in an ever-changing landscape of challenges. Effectiveness is often inefficient, usually messy, and always short-lived, such that a system that works for one era may not work for another.

Predictive → Adaptive

In the old Enlightenment and the machine age that followed, inputs were assumed to predict outputs. In the second Enlightenment, once we recognize that the laws that govern the world are laws of complex systems, we must trade the story of inputs and predictability for a story of influence and ever-shifting adaptation. In complex human societies, individuals act and adapt to changing circumstances; their adaptations in turn influence the next round of action, and so on. This picture of how neither risks nor outcomes can be fully anticipated makes flexibility and resilience more valuable at every scale of decision-making.

Independent → Interdependent

The Enlightenment allowed us to see ourselves as individuals and agents. Free from supernatural authority, people were first allowed and then expected to act independently and selfishly for themselves. This extraordinary cultural shift sparked invention, innovation, and the autonomy we expect in our daily lives. But this mode of thinking, particularly applied to the American frontier, persuaded us that we were independent rather than inter-dependent. A new understanding of systems and human behavior and physiology shows this to be untrue. From the quantum level up, we are far more interdependent than our politics and culture generally let us think. We are at all times both cause and effect. Our mirror neurons and evolved social rites mean that how we behave influences how others behave, and how they behave influences us. The permutating patterns formed by those interactions become the shape our societies take. And obviously, the denser and more connected the network—compare, say, America today with America 300 years ago—the greater these effects.

Rational calculator → Irrational approximators

The Enlightenment encouraged scientists to apply math-ematics and physics to human nature and social dynamics, but these were of course blunt instruments for such com-plex work, requiring many simplifying assumptions. Over time, the caveat that these assumptions were simplify-ing fell away and what was left was a mechanical view that people are rational calculators of their own interest. Economists even today assume that an ordinary consumer can make complex instantaneous calculations about net present value and risk when making decisions in grocery stores between tomatoes and carrots. This *homo economicus* stands at the center of traditional economics, and his predilection for perfect rationality and selfishness permeates our politics and culture. By contrast, the behavioral science of our times is pulling us back to common sense and reminding us that people are often irrational or at least a-rational and emotional, and that we are at best approximators of interest who often don't know what's best for us and even when we do, often don't do it. This accounts for the "animal spirits" of fear, longing, and greed that seem to drive markets in unpredictable and irrational ways.

Selfish → Strongly reciprocal

For centuries, a bedrock economic, legal, and social assumption was that people were inherently so selfish that they could not be expected to support or aid others not in their own genetic line. Now the study of human behavior reinforces the neglected fact that we are hardwired equally to be cooperative. As social psychologist Dacher Keltner writes in *Born to Be Good*, humans could not have survived and evolved without the social organization that only cooperation, mutuality, and reciprocity make possible. In fact, we are so tilted toward cooperation that we punish non-cooperators in our communities, even at cost to ourselves. This "strong reciprocation" strategy reflects a deep recognition, made instinctual through millennia of group activity, that all behavior is contagious, and that rewarding good with good and bad with punishment is the best way to protect our societies and therefore ourselves. Reciprocity makes compassion not a form of weakness but a model of strength; it makes pro-social morality not just moral but natural and smart.

Win-lose → Win-win or lose-lose

The story that grew out of Enlightenment rationalism and then Social Darwinism had a strong streak of "your gain is my loss." The more that people and groups were seen as competing isles of ambition, all struggling for survival, the more life was analogized at every turn into a win-lose scenario. But the stories and science of the second Enlightenment prove what has long been a parallel intuition: that in fact, the evolution of humanity from cave dweller to Facebooker is the story of increasing adoption of nonzero, or positive-sum, attitudes; and that societies capable of setting up win-win (or lose-lose) scenarios always win. Robert Wright's *Nonzero* describes this dynamic across civilizations. Unhealthy societies think zero-sum and fight over a pie of fixed size. Healthy societies think 1+1=3 and operate from a norm that the pie can grow. Open, non-equilibrium systems have synergies that generate increasing returns and make the whole greater than the sum of the parts. The proper goal of politics and economics is to maximize those increasing returns and win-win scenarios.

Competition → Cooperation

A fundamental assumption of traditional economics is that competitiveness creates prosperity. This view, descended from a misreading of Adam Smith and Charles Darwin, weds the invisible hand of the market to the natural selection of nature. It justifies atomistic self-seeking. A clearer understanding of how evolutionary forces work in a complex adaptive human society shows that *cooperation* is the true foundation of prosperity (as does a full reading of Adam Smith's lesser-known master-piece *A Theory of Moral Sentiments*). Competition properly understood—in nature or in business—is between groups of cooperators. Groups that know how to cooperate—whose members attend to social and emotional skills like empathy—defeat those that do not. That's because only cooperation can create symbiotic, nonzero outcomes. And those nonzero outcomes, borne and propelled by ever-increasing trust and cooperation, create a feedback loop of ever-increasing economic growth and social health.

Now: what does all this have to do with self-interest?

Everything. Our previous understanding of the world animated and enabled a primitive and narrow perspective on self-interest, giving us such notions as:

–I should be able to do whatever I please, so long as it doesn't directly harm someone else.

–Your loss is my gain.

–It's survival of the fittest—only the strong survive.

–Rugged individualism wins.

–We are a nation of self-made people.

–Every man for himself.

Until recently, these beliefs—we aptly call them "rational-izations"—could be backed, even if speciously, by refer-ences to science and laws of nature. But now, to anyone really paying attention, they can't. Today, emerging from our knowledge of emergence, complexity, and innate human behavior, a different story about self-interest is taking shape, and it sounds more like this:

–What goes around comes around.

–The better you do, the better I do.

–It's survival of the smartest—only the cooperative survive.

–Teamwork wins.

–There's no such thing as a self-made person.

–All for one, one for all.

Let's be clear here: we are not talking about a sudden embrace of saintly self-denial. We are talking about humans correcting their vision—as they did when they recognized that the sun didn't orbit the earth; as they did when they acknowledged that germs, not humours, caused sickness. We are talking about humans seeing, with long-overdue clarity, and with all our millennia of self-preservation instincts intact, a simple truth: *True self-interest is mutual interest.* The best way to improve your likelihood of surviving and thriving is to make sure those around you survive and thrive. Notwithstanding American mythology about selfishness making the world go round, humans have in fact evolved—*have been selected*—to look out for others in their group and, in so doing, to look out for self. We exist today because this is how our ancestors behaved. We evolve today by ensuring that our definition of "our group" is wide enough to take advantage of diversity and narrow enough to be actionable.

This is a story, in short, about self-interest that is smart, or "self-interest properly understood," as Tocqueville put it. It is a true story. It tells of neither altruism nor raw simple selfishness. Altruism is admirable, but not common enough to support a durable moral or political system. Raw selfishness may seem like the savvy stance, but is in fact self-defeating: tragedies of the commons are so called because they kill first the commons and then the people. True self-interest is mutual interest. This is even more urgently true in the age of global climate change, terror, drugs, pop culture, marketing, and so forth than it was in the age of hunter-gatherers.

We are aware that many have used the "newest science" to justify outlandish views and schemes, or to lend a patina of certainty to things ineffable. It would be easy to characterize our reliance on new science as similarly naïve. We are also aware, acutely, that the Machinebrain thinking we criticize is itself the direct product of science, and that our remedy may appear strangely to be a fresh dose of the illness. But while skepticism is warranted, there is an important difference: today's science is most useful in how it demonstrates *the limits of science.* Complexity theory doesn't give you mastery over the systems we inhabit; it simply informs us about their inherent unpredictability and instability. These new perspectives should not make us more certain of our approaches, but rather, more keenly aware of how our approaches can go wrong or become outmoded, and how necessary it is in civic life to be able to adjust to changes in fact and experience.

Where the rationalist schemes of central planners on the left and market fundamentalists on the right have led to costly hubris, public policy informed by the new science should now lead to constant *humility.*

In a sense, the latest wave of scientific understanding merely confirms what we, in our bones, know to be true: that no one is an island; and that someone who thinks he can take for himself, everyone else be damned, causes a society to become too sick to sustain anyone. Indeed, he or she who defers his own immediate gain, for either the longer term or the greater good, causes a society to prosper so much as to pay back his investment of deferred gratification. True self-interest is mutual interest.

The contrast between the new and old stories of self-interest —like any paradigmatic shift in public imagination—is not just a philosophical curiosity. It plays out in how we interpret and understand—and therefore, prepare for or prevent— calamities like global financial meltdowns or catastrophic climate change or political gridlock. And it will transform the way we think about three basic elements of a democratic society: citizenship, economy, government.

What does it mean to be a citizen, to live in public, to be a contributing and effective member of a community? What is the purpose of an economy, and how, in a free society, can the market work to serve *all* people? And what is government for? As will become clear in the coming pages, we think of citizenship, the economy, and the government as living ecosystems—as gardens rather than machines, requiring a holistic sense of interconnectedness, rewarding both humility and active responsibility.

We begin, in the next chapter, with great citizenship.

III. Great Citizenship

Society Becomes How You Behave

Why "It's not my problem" is a problem and why too many people think citizenship is for suckers—Both the market and the state have crowded out citizenship, reducing it to a cramped and crabby consumerism—The intellectual foundation of our old idea of citizenship is outmoded—A new basis for understanding healthy civic life, drawn from the science and reality of interdependence and contagion—Citizens as gardeners: five rules for great citizenship

TOO OFTEN IN AMERICA TODAY, to call someone a good citizen is to treat her like a saint who's gone to some special length to help another—or like a sucker who forgot to look out for herself.

Either way, what's assumed so much of the time is that being a good citizen is something either beyond or against self-interest. The very word "citizenship" has a musty, 1950s feel to it, evoking a time when people tried hard to be seen as pro-social, when scouts got badges for it. The memory of that time can stir nostalgia or disparagement. But it does often seem like that time has passed.

America has high rates of volunteerism and charity and we respond swiftly to disasters at home and abroad. But at the same time, too many Americans today live their everyday lives by an ethic of "that's not my problem." The "not my problem" mindset is a problem. It is both the source and the result of an ideology that exalts individual autonomy at all costs. It is also, as we will explain below, highly contagious and quickly corrosive. And thus it is part of a feedback loop in which the disavowal of problems creates the very problems being disavowed.

Our argument in this chapter is that there's no such thing as "not my problem." We don't mean that all problems are equal or equally our burden, which would be paralyzing. We mean simply that great citizenship treats civic life as a garden demanding constant tending and the willingness to see all problems as interconnected.

It is an accepted axiom of corporate life that great companies create a culture where any problem the company faces is every employee's problem. These are cultures where employees compete to identify and solve problems, rather than avoid them. In this way, problems are quickly identified and solved, or even better, headed off completely. By contrast, a corporate culture where problems are avoided or blamed on others inevitably leads to infighting, suboptimization, and failure.

So it seems obvious to us that we must create a civic culture that mirrors such high-performance organizational cultures—where every problem the society faces is everyone's problem. As we will explain below, a culture where every problem is everyone's problem predictably has very few problems.

The Squeeze on Citizenship

In too many American communities today, such a culture of civic ownership does not prevail. Robert Putnam has documented the decades-long decimation of Tocqueville's little platoons of democracy, the voluntary associations from bowling leagues to Elks clubs that once comprised a vibrant civic ecosystem. National measures of civic health—from volunteering to neighborliness to social connectedness—have all declined substantially since the 1970s.

All around us, in less measurable ways, there has been a slow and quiet seepage of trust and responsibility. For instance, not until you stop and think about it might this seem odd: today we have a federal law requiring chief executives of public corporations to declare affirmatively in their corporate reports that they are not lying. Perhaps you find it outrageous that private security guards in a public bus tunnel in Seattle would stand by and watch a vicious beating of one teenager by another—and that the guards would justify their passivity by pointing out that the law forbade them from intervening like police officers. But then you move on. This is how it is.

The two of us don't believe that great citizenship has been killed just yet. We do believe, however, that it has been crowded out—by the market on one side and by the state on the other. Nowadays, too many people think of their responsibilities of citizenship as limited mainly to basic compliance with the law, or perhaps jury duty or voting—and, of course, only half of us even vote.

The market is the first force that has led to the shriveling of citizenship. The classic case is the Wal-Mart effect. A town has a Main Street of small businesses and mom-and-pop shops. The shopkeepers and their customers have relationships that are not just about economic transactions but are set in a context of family, neighborhood, people, and place. Then Wal-Mart comes to town. It offers lower prices. It offers convenience. Because of its scale and might in the marketplace, it can compensate its workers stingily and drive out competition.

The presence of Wal-Mart leads the townspeople to think of themselves primarily as consumers, and to shed other aspects of their identities, like being neighbors or parishioners or friends. As consumers first, they gravitate to the place with the lowest prices. Wal-Mart thrives. The small businesses struggle and lay off workers. They cut back on their sponsorship of tee ball, their support of the food bank. As the mom-and-pops give way to the big box, and commutes become necessary, lives become more frenetic and stressful. People see each other less often. The sense of mutual obligation that townsfolk once shared starts to evaporate. Microhabits of caring and sociability fall away. In this tableau of libertarian citizenship, market forces triumph and everyone gets better deals—yet everyone is now in many senses poorer.

Two things have happened in such a scene, which, by the way, is not about Wal-Mart alone but about an ideology that treats everything—including people—like costs to be reduced. When we see ourselves as consumers above all, we start thinking of citizenship as grumpy customerhood—as suspicious, skeptical, "what's-in-it-for-me" consumerism. Globalization and pressures on the middle class accelerate these effects. Throw in the scarcity mindset and anxieties of the Great Recession and the harm compounds. The insidious marketization of life distorts—indeed, corrupts—our politics and our civic lives.

Meanwhile, on another front, the state has encroached increasingly into arenas of civic action, reducing the space that people have to show up for one another. What used to be the sort of thing you or I might just do because it needed doing, we now see as someone else's job. What used to be left to common sense is now prescribed by law. What used to be undertaken by self-organizing citizens is now too often delegated to the state. Elinor Ostrom's classic *Governing the Commons* depicts these dynamics in societies around the world.

But for direct evidence we need examine only our own schools. Somewhere between the one-room schoolhouse of the 19th century and the assembly-line high school of the 20th, Americans came to accept the tacit notion that the walls of the school are to keep kids in and others out. As public education has become more bureaucratized and rule-bound, and the actual work of teaching more test-driven, it's become easier for parents to drop their children off and check out of the process of education. At the same time, it's become harder for parents—or, for that matter, neighbors or grandparents or mentors—to enter the classroom and become a truly integrated part of the schooling experience, let alone to improve the actual quality of the school.

A norm now prevails in most public schools that education is the job of professional educators. Rules have arisen to support that norm. There were probably good reasons for such rules, and certainly teachers are professionals to be respected. But one unintended consequence of all this is that the state gives us permission to treat education— even of one's own child—as someone else's job (or problem). When challenges arise in a public school, it's rare or only on the margins that families or the community are permitted to come up with solutions or innovations.

What's lost in such crowding-out and such shifts of power?

Quality of life, for one thing. In the case of the decimated Main Street, the glue of neighborliness disappears when everyone drives to the superstore. Eye contact, touch, presence, and smiles: all decline and disappear. In the case of the school-as-fortress, children get a desiccated experience of what it means to live in community. No adult outside the school owes them any special support or concern, and they in turn don't owe any back. Our schools are worse for it.

What's lost is the willingness of people to make judgments in situations that are not formulaic but are messy and human, and then to trust each other to make the best calls we can. As Philip Howard has argued powerfully, in a society that over-relies on laws and rules to govern everyday interactions—one where much is prescribed and proscribed and "what is not prohibited is permitted"—people forget how to exercise both rights and responsibilities.

What's lost, in short, is citizenship. By "citizenship" we do not mean legal documentation status. We mean living in a pro-social way at every scale of life. We mean showing up for each other.

Citizenship matters because it delivers for society what neither the market nor the state can or should. Citizenship isn't just voting. Nor is it just Good Samaritanism. A 21st-century perspective forces us to acknowledge that citizenship is, quite simply, the work of being in public. It encompasses behaviors like courtesy and civility, the "etiquette of freedom," to use poet Gary Snyder's phrase. It encompasses small acts like teaching your children to be honest in their dealings with others. It includes serving on community councils and as soccer coaches. It means leaving a place in better shape than you found it. It means helping others during hard times and being able to ask for help. It means resisting the temptation to call a problem someone else's.

Central to our conception of citizenship is an ethic of sacrifice—and a belief that sacrifice should be *progressive*. That is to say, being a citizen is not just about serving others and contributing when it's convenient but also when it's inconvenient. And the scale of the contribution should grow in proportion to the ability of the person to contribute. Just as progressive taxation asks those who can pull the most weight to do so, progressive civic contribution asks those who have the most civic capacity— and who have benefited most from our civic culture—to take the most responsibility.

Citizen Gardeners

In the opening section of this book, we laid out a new story of self-interest. It is an obliteration of the myth of rugged individualism. The self-made person may be a great American icon but he is also a fairy tale. Ask that individualist who made the bootstraps she is pulling up. Ask her who paved the road that she walked on to be able to see you, who taught her the very language she uses to assert her independence.

Citizenship is a recognition that we are interdependent— that there are values, systems, and skills that hold us together as social animals, particularly in a tolerant, multi-ethnic market democracy. More than that, citizenship is a rejection of what Francis Fukuyama has labeled "the

Hobbesian fallacy," the ahistorical notion that humans began as individuals and only later rationally calculated that it made sense to band together in society. In fact, humans have been social from very the start; individualism is a creation of recent centuries.

The old story of self-interest is a product—and perpetuator—of Machinebrain. The new story is an exemplar of Gardenbrain.

Machinebrain held that citizens are automatons, mindlessly seeking advantage over one another, colliding like billiard balls, and that the best to be hoped for in civic life is that we should channel our irredeemable self-seeking into a machinery of checks and balances that can set one interest or faction against another. Machinebrain uses malevolence to cancel out malevolence in the hopes of generating benevolence. This is the political and civic culture that has dominated American politics since the early 19th century.

Gardenbrain, by contrast, sees citizens as gardeners, tending to the plots we share—and also as organisms within a greater garden, each affecting the next. We form each other. We are bound up in each other's choices. We are not separate. As Paul said in Corinthians, "the eye cannot say unto the hand, I have no need of thee: nor again the head to the feet, I have no need of you." We are deeply, irretrievably interdependent. We cannot pretend that our acts and choices happen in isolation. When we start with this recognition, we have to accept more responsibility. For everything.

If this sounds weird to you, perhaps that is because you live in a society that is, to use the acronym coined by moral psychologist Jonathan Haidt, WEIRD: Western, educated, industrialized, rich, and democratic. In other parts of the world, Haidt shows in *The Righteous Mind*, people have always paid far more attention than we Americans do to relationships among things and people than to the separateness of all objects. Gardenbrain sees systems. It tempers autonomy with community.

Creating Civic Contagions

Yet Gardenbrain also enables us to claim more individual power—much more power than conventional theories of citizenship attribute to us as individuals. For one of the central facts of life on an interdependent web is that every action and omission is potentially powerfully contagious. When you are compassionate and generous, society can become compassionate and generous. When you are violent and hateful, society can become violent and hateful. *You* can be the original cause of that contagion.

Why? Because humans are copying machines. As the philosopher Eric Hoffer once said, "When people are free to do as they please, they usually imitate each other." What this means is not that you are powerless but that you can set off a new chain of copying—and you do—every day with every act.

In their groundbreaking book on social networks, *Connected*, Nicholas Christakis and James Fowler document the powerful and remarkable effect social networks have on us, and we on them. Exploring a variety of social phenomena, from obesity to home-buying to happiness, Christakis and Fowler show that "social networks affect every aspect of our lives. Events occurring in distant others can determine the shape of our lives, what we think, what we desire, whether we fall ill or die."

This is to be taken not as generalized ethical precept but rather as a reporting of social fact. Just because you don't immediately, or perhaps ever, see the virus of behavior leap from host to host doesn't mean it isn't leaping. It is, relentlessly. Most people are wired for strong reciprocity, which means we repay good with good and bad with bad, and are willing to repay bad with bad even at some personal cost, just to reinforce group norms.

As a result, even when good behavior is the minority choice in a bad setting, those who hew to good behavior can eventually prevail—and they are not suckers for doing so, but rather players of the long game over the short.

This law of enlightened citizenship also makes it insufficient

CITIZENSHIP: *Machinebrain View*

If everyone just
does what's best for self,
society will be OK

I should be able to
do whatever I please
as long as it does not
harm others directly

People are
rational and selfish

Success is a result
of individual effort

I'm an island

I am self-made

I am autonomous—
an independent
thinker and actor

My behavior
is isolated

I shouldn't have to
worry about other
people's problems

Cooperation is
a necessary evil

Individuals
precede society

**Humans are
intrinsically
individualistic**

Service to others
is nice but not
necessary

Trust is
for suckers

Every man
for himself

What I do is no one's
business but my own and
does not affect others

CITIZENSHIP: *Gardenbrain View*

If we act as if we are reliant on one another, society will be OK

People are emotional and reciprocal

Individual effort and contribution matter only in the setting of a community

Humans are intrinsically social

Success is the result of cooperating to compete

I'm a node on a network

I'm influencing others — we are all interconnected and interdependent

I am shaped in great measure by my context

Other people's problems will eventually be my problem

Only sociopaths do
whatever they please

Cooperation
is essential

Society
precedes the
individual

Service to others is
reciprocity, which makes
the world work

We're all in
it together

Trust is what makes
strong economies and
nations

My behavior is
contagious — society
becomes how I behave

Everything I do
(and don't do)
affects others

for us merely to complain about social trends we don't like. When you read in the news about teenage pregnancies or greedy Wall Street CEOs or steroid-taking athletes, you cannot say that those people are bringing America down. You cannot distance yourself from the trend that you decry. You own it—either because you contributed to that contagion or because you didn't contribute enough to stopping it. Either way, permission from someone else for you to act was never required.

Understanding the world as networked, complex, and adaptive frames our perspective. Any human population will have a wide range of behaviors, from completely altruistic to totally sociopathic. Some people will be criminal and dishonest, many others will simply be what social scientists call "free riders." Free riders accept the benefits of their environment without being willing to pay the costs to create those benefits. This is well understood. What is now just as well understood is the destabilizing effect their behavior has on the group. Free riders gain initial competitive advantage over non-free riders, and thus put pressure on them. Companies that are allowed to cheat destroy industries by forcing all competitors into a race to the bottom. People who are free riders destroy communities by forcing citizens into the same behaviors.

Anti-social contagions spread more readily than pro-social ones, for the same reason that it is easier to push things downhill than up, and easier to fall into vice than into virtue. The challenge is how to generate the right kinds of contagions.

Five Rules

There are five rules we lay out for pro-social citizenship, and they reflect our epidemiological way of looking at civic life.

Small acts of leadership compound. Participating in a town meeting on a proposed new highway. Leading a corps of afterschool reading tutors. Persuading other voters to support a ballot measure. These are forms of citizenship. So is turning off a running faucet. Picking up a candy wrapper. Helping someone with a heavy load. True citizenship is about treating even the most trivial choice as a chance to shape your society and be a leader. It is laying down habits that scale up throughout society. It is not just setting an example; it is actively leading others to copy you. The science of complex adaptive systems teaches us that small acts, tiny everyday choices, accrue and compound into tipping points. We believe that the systems of the body politic, like the systems of the human body, are fractally interrelated. Just as the tiniest capillaries ramify into like-shaped webs of arteries, so too do the smallest pathways of civic action yield similar patterns of politics and common life. Tiny acts of responsibility are replicated, scale upon scale, and thus every act is inherently an act of leadership—either in a pro-social or anti-social way. Every one of us can set off a cascade. Understood thus, the habits and culture of citizenship aren't good for social health; they are essential for it. In schools, homes, firms, and every domain, adults have to be more comfortable talking about and modeling *character* in the most modest-seeming of acts. And as we will discuss more below, government at every turn should be helping citizens take responsibility in small ways too.

Infect the supercarriers. If we look at good citizenship as a contagion, but as a contagion we want to accelerate rather than contain, then it behooves us to search out the supercarriers—the nodes of networks in every community whose influence and reach are disproportionate. Then it behooves us to infect them. We ensure that they model the kind of pro-social behavior we want, talk about it, and reward it in their own networks. The supercarriers need not be the obvious and most visible leaders; in every circle, there are those who, regardless of station, are so trusted by others that they can make a meme spread very rapidly. Whether you are a neighborhood activist or a youth organizer or a marketer, it has become more necessary than ever to learn and to teach the skills of reading network maps, identifying the nodes, and developing educational and other persuasive strategies for activating those nodes.

Bridge more than bond. For some Americans, citizenship is expressed by clustering with people very much like oneself. There's of course a fulfilling place for that in life. But we believe in what Mark Granovetter called "the strength of weak ties." What sustains the ecosystem of citizenship is not reinforcing old and already strong ties with, say, fellow liberals or soccer fans or Brooklynites, but instead building new and somewhat weaker ties with conservatives or baseball fans or Manhattanites. In every latticework, whether chemical or physical or human, it's the links that connect a tight ring to another tight ring that add the greatest collective value and make the network bigger and more powerful. Or to put it in terms used by Robert Putnam, *bridging* social capital is better than *bonding*. Great citizens build bridges between unacquainted realms, more than they reinforce bonds among people already close. Bridging spreads trust while bonding concentrates it. This is why, as Putnam described long before he wrote of "bowling alone," southern Italy with its more tribal blood loyalties has long been a less functional and prosperous social milieu than northern Italy, where weak ties and openness prevail. But because people tend naturally toward building strong ties, they often have to be encouraged to develop the habit of creating weaker ones. In this light, programs like a universal draft or required national civilian service are necessary for diverse democracies. These experiences connect us in ways that the tribalism of everyday life does not.

Create Dunbar units. We believe that one of the great forces that feeds both citizen apathy and the citizen rage of the Tea Party phenomenon is bigness, and the power-lessness it engenders: big government fighting big business as reported by big media, all fueled by big money, and leaving most of us on the sidelines. The antidote is smallness. Our vision of citizenship is moral and philo-sophical, but it comes to life only on a face-to-face human scale. There is reason why, across all cultures and time periods, the maximum size of a coherent community has always been about 150. This is known as Dunbar's num-ber, after the social scientist Robin Dunbar, who named the phenomenon. As a matter of both public policy and private self-organization, we should be de-chunking our-selves into units of no more than 150, and then connect-ing the chunks. A neighborhood or a housing project of 1000 units is not really a neighborhood. A neighborhood consisting of 10 sets of 100 houses, each set linked to the others—that's more like it. Since vast cities and vast national organizations create deserts of citizenship, we believe in localizing globally—every chance we get, mak-ing little Dunbar units and getting them to identify as such, bridging with one another, sometimes competing in a healthy way with one another. When one's civic action consists of being just a dues-paying member of a vast national organization, one is only a fraction as powerful and empowered as when it consists of being a leader in a local network, particularly one tied to other local networks. A small-town ethos situated in a high-tech web—as found, for instance, in the statewide network of Watershed Councils in Oregon—makes for effective 21st-century citizenship.

Make courtesy count. Courtesy—a cooperative consideration of, and deferral to, the needs of others—is the start of true citizenship. It is what we practice when we don't live on an island alone. And that is why we believe courtesy should be actively encouraged in American civic life, not as ritual or routine but as mindful practice. When you open doors for others, let others into traffic, say "please" and "thank you," you are watering the garden of social life. These kinds of choices can be named and promoted. Though courtesy connotes something courtly and quaint, it is actually one of the most vital and fluid forces in any civic ecology. That is because, at bottom, courtesy is about subordinating the self, even if momentarily. It breeds trust, and trust is everything in civic life.

Trust in trust. Trust is foremost among the social virtues that make healthy societies. Alas, we note its absence more readily than its presence. When market actors behave in ways that erode the trust that citizens have in one another—as Wall Street banks did in peddling financial time bombs during the housing boom—they send a signal that "dumb money" deserves its fate. When the state acts in ways that erode the trust that citizens have in one another—by codifying a presumption of deceptiveness, as the CEO affirmations do, or by requiring teachers to teach certain pages of a text on certain days—it is not just responding to a depletion of trust; it's contributing to it. By contrast, every act of great citizenship adds to the social stocks of trust. Designing experiences where people come to know each other, where they can expect to encounter one another repeatedly, and where the quality of life is increased for all if each individual thinks of himself as a steward—or trustee—of the experience: this is what life is like, say, in a neighborhood library branch, and we believe great citizens behave as if every space they are in is a public library.

Trust, in short, is the DNA to be found in all the other habits of citizenship. It is what fuels the fractal impact of small acts of leadership. It is what empowers supercarriers to infect others. It is what makes weak ties useful. It is why we need to preserve a human scale for citizenship. And it is why courtesy counts.

The Power of One

We recognize that there are latent dangers in the networked ethics we advocate. One is what might be called "hivemind," the tendency for individuals to lose their voice and identity in the midst of the collective. The other is simple bullying, the fear the Framers had in mind when they drafted the Constitution, that majorities might create great waves of opinion that swamp minorities.

As to the first fear, we are no champions of group-driven dehumanization. But citizenship of the kind we describe is the *opposite* of dehumanizing conformity. When any one person can be an agent of contagion, and can set off cascades of new thought or action, that is a truly empowering situation. Yes, that one person needs to have some savvy about how complex systems tip, and not everyone has that. But the fact is that in our story of citizenship, the individual has even more power than she does in the more atomized, solipsistic account of citizenship—and far more than in some collectivist dystopia. The corollary to always being influenced by others (which we are) is always being able to influence others—a power we dramatically underutilize.

As to the second fear, of majoritarian bullying, what we value is cooperation, and there is a crucial distinction between cooperation and conformity. Cooperation presumes difference—and derives its moral value from the fact that joint action is undertaken out of difference rather than out of sameness. That said, we do believe it's perfectly appropriate for majorities to squeeze out anti-social behavior. The trick is being clear about what constitutes anti- and pro-social behavior. By anti-social we do not mean "deviant" and "unlike others," as communism or homosexuality were once tagged. We mean behavior that is pathologically selfish, that breaks down group trust and cooperation in pursuit of egotism.

How *You* Behave

When one person behaves like it's OK to litter, others do as well, and the behavior of littering goes viral. Or take another example. You're at the park enjoying a picnic with family and friends and a boom box. Another group at a nearby table turns up their music. Now you feel you've got to turn up your music so that it isn't drowned out. Then the other group feels the same, and turns up *their* music.

In the study of sound they call this the Lombard effect, the ratcheting-up of noise levels as everyone fights to be heard over the din of everyone else. There is a civic Lombard effect as well. And in a world where the operating mode is to do what you want to do, damn the consequences to anyone else, we get Lombard-esque cycles of discourtesy and disregard.

The new science we spoke of in the introduction reveals that in a networked environment, where behaviors are contagious and can lead to cascades of anti-social one-upmanship, there is only one way to stop the spiral. And that is to stop the spiral. Or to put it another way, it is to recognize that *society becomes how you behave*—not anyone else but you.

This is a deceptively profound idea. To assume that society becomes how you behave is to leave behind forever the myth of social externalities—that you don't have to bear the costs of your bad or selfish behavior. To assume that society becomes how you behave is to leave behind also the myth that you are just one in a billion, that somewhere out there is some good person whose acts can cancel out your bad ones, thus creating no net social harm.

To assume that society becomes how you behave is to take on the responsibility of everyday "small l" leadership. This is more than acknowledging that on an individual basis, character counts and virtue matters. It's acting as if the character of a community will, sooner or later, *exactly* reflect your own character: because it will. Collective character is real and something each of us shapes.

So, for instance, when you are cut off in traffic and feel the chemical rush of road rage, play out two scenarios. The first is the commonly expected one, in which the rest of your drive is dedicated to exacting revenge against the offending driver or to paying his ruthlessness forward and cutting off another driver.

The alternative scenario is one in which you catch yourself and choose not to compound one person's discourtesy with your own. Here, you recognize that if you make the small decision to let drivers into traffic, even if it feels like an affront to your dignity, then other people will do the same.

Because the first scenario is indeed the common one, and everyone assumes its rules are the rules of the freeway, gridlock and awful traffic jams are the inevitable result. But when we let the second scenario play out, traffic flows more smoothly. Gridlock does not occur. We get where we want to get faster.

This is not just parable. It is hard science. People who study complex adaptive systems—using computer models of traffic going along two axes (north-south and east-west)—can demonstrate and compare the effects of these two scenarios. Lesson one: others will act the way you act. Lesson two: when you act in a pro-social way, the net result for you and everyone else is better.

This may seem counterintuitive, the notion that slowing down gets you there faster, that to yield now is to advance later. The reason, again, is our ingrained and too-narrow idea about what constitutes our self-interest. In a one-time transaction with someone who won't exist after the transaction (and here, we are describing the parameters of neoclassical economics), you might rightly think that screwing that person is the best way to achieve your own interest. At a minimum, you'd be safe to think you could get away with it. You would think that someone else's problem is someone else's problem.

If, however, we allow for the possibility that the other person in the transaction may still exist after the transaction,

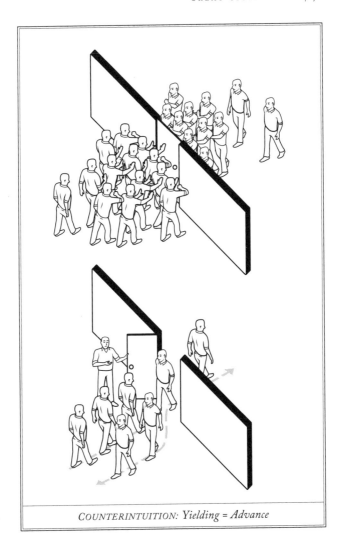

COUNTERINTUITION: Yielding = Advance

then we think differently. If we allow for the possibility that the other person will not only reciprocate vis-à-vis you but will also carry your behavior virally to others, then we must act differently. If we allow for the possibility that someone else's problem is eventually your problem too, then we must act differently.

This possibility is called real life.

We acknowledge that this vision of true citizenship is challenging. The picture we paint here is not of the path of least resistance. Our vision requires people to lean forward and engage rather than lean back and let things happen. Left to themselves, many Americans—indeed, most humans—choose convenience over participation. But while it seems convenient to cede responsibility for the common good to the market or the state, that convenience is penny-wise and pound-foolish. It diminishes our feeling of enfranchisement, and our actual power. And while it seems inconvenient to show up and participate, that inconvenience pays dividends in material benefit and in the purposeful enjoyment of life. Why? Because participation, freely chosen rather than incentivized or delegated, springs from intrinsic motivation—and intrinsic motivation yields the kind of happiness that money can't buy and laws can't create.

To us, however, the most challenging aspect of what we call true citizenship is that it requires us to be continuously aware and alert to the ways in which both the market and the state tend to crowd out citizenship in ways that are gradual and often imperceptible, like the boiling of the proverbial frog.

We are not anti-market or anti-government. As our critics on both the left and the right will discover to their frustration in the pages to come, we are for both vibrant capitalism and an activist government. And we believe there is a vital role for both market and state in fostering true citizenship. That role consists not only in getting out of the way but also in designing choice architectures and signal-sending environments that crowd out the bad and crowd in the good. But ultimately, it all comes down to very intensely personal choices—to be mindful, continuously, of our power and obligation as sources of social contagion. To live with St. Paul's words in our hearts—or not. To weed the bad and seed the good, like great gardeners.

Society becomes how *you* behave.

And whether the market and government reinforce great citizenship, or undermine it, will be the focus of the next two chapters of this book.

IV. True Capitalism

*We're All Better Off When
We're All Better Off*

*The efficient market hypothesis, market fundamentalism,
and the costs of the prevailing idea of what an
economy is—The alternative and evolutionary vision:
the market as garden—Trickle-down economics
and the war on the middle class—Middle-out
economics, and the way forward*

THIS BOOK WAS CONCEIVED in the wake of the most significant financial crisis since the Great Depression. During 2007 and 2008, giant financial institutions were obliterated, the net worth of most Americans collapsed, and most of the world's economies were brought to their knees.

At the same time, this has been an era of radical economic inequality, at levels not seen since 1929. Over the last three decades, an unprecedented consolidation and concentration of earning power and wealth has made the top 1 percent of Americans immensely richer while middle-class Americans have been increasingly impoverished.

To most Americans and certainly most economists and policymakers, these two phenomena seem unrelated. In fact, traditional economic theory and contemporary American economic policy does not seem to admit the possibility that they are connected in any way.

And yet they are—deeply. In the following pages we aim to show that a modern understanding of economies as complex, adaptive, interconnected systems forces us to conclude that radical inequality and radical economic dislocation are causally linked: one brings and amplifies the other.

If we want a high-growth society with broadly shared prosperity, and if we want to avoid dislocations like the one we have just gone through, we need to change our theory of action foundationally. We need to stop thinking about the economy as a perfect, self-correcting machine and start thinking of it as a garden.

Traditional economic theory is rooted in a 19th- and 20th-century understanding of science and mathematics. At the simplest level, traditional theory assumes economies are linear systems filled with rational actors who seek to optimize their situation. Outputs reflect a sum of inputs, the system is closed, and if big change comes it comes as an external shock. The system's default state is equilibrium. The prevailing metaphor is a machine.

But this is not how economies are. It never has been. As anyone can see and feel today, economies behave in ways that are non-linear and irrational, and often violently so. These often-violent changes are not external shocks but emergent properties—the *inevitable* result—of the way economies behave.

The traditional approach, in short, completely misunderstands human behavior and natural economic forces. The problem is that the traditional model is not an academic curiosity; it is the basis for an ideological story about the economy and government's role—and that story has fueled policymaking and morphed into a selfishness-justifying conventional wisdom.

Even today, the debate between free marketeers and Keynesians unfolds on the terms of the market fundamentalists: government stimulus efforts are usually justified as a way to restore equilibrium, and defended as regrettable deviations from government's naturally minimalist role.

Fortunately, as we've described above, it is now possible to understand and describe economic systems as complex systems like gardens. And it is now reasonable to assert that economic systems are not merely similar to ecosystems; they are ecosystems, driven by the same types of evolutionary forces as ecosystems. Eric Beinhocker's *The Origin of Wealth* is the most lucid survey available of this new complexity economics.

The story Beinhocker tells is simple, and not unlike the story Darwin tells. In an economy, as in any ecosystem, innovation is the result of evolutionary and competitive pressures. Within any given competitive environment—or what's called a "fitness landscape"—individuals and groups cooperate to compete, to find solutions to problems and share the gains from those solutions. The most successful strategies for cooperation spread and multiply. Throughout, minor initial advantages get amplified and locked in—as do disadvantages. Whether you are predator or prey, spore or seed, the opportunity to thrive compounds and then *concentrates*. It bunches. It never stays evenly spread.

Like a garden, the economy consists of an environment and interdependent elements—sun, soil, seed, water. But far more than a garden, the economy also contains the expectations and interpretations all the agents have about what all the *other* agents want and expect. And that invisible web of human expectations becomes, in an ever-amplifying spiral, both cause and effect of external circumstances. Thus the housing-led financial crisis. Complexity scientists describe it in terms of "feedback loops." Financier George Soros has described it as "reflexivity." What I think you think about what I want creates storms of behavior that change *what is*.

Traditional economics holds that the economy is an equilibrium system; that things tend, over time, to even out and return to "normal." Complexity economics shows that the economy, like a garden, is never in perfect balance or stasis and is always both growing and shrinking. And like an untended garden, an economy left entirely to itself tends toward unhealthy imbalances. This is a very different starting point, and it leads to very different conclusions about what the government should do about the economy.

Einstein said, "Make everything as simple as possible, but not too simple." The problem with traditional economics is that it has made things too simple and then compounded the error by treating the oversimplification as gospel. The bedrock assumption of traditional economic theory and conventional economic wisdom is that markets are perfectly efficient and therefore self-correcting. This "efficient market hypothesis," born of the machine-age obsession with the physics of perfect mechanisms, is hard to square with intuition and reality—harder for laypeople than for economic experts. And yet, like a dead hand on the wheel, the efficient market hypothesis still drives everything in economic policymaking.

Consider that if markets are perfectly efficient then it *must* be true that:

–The market is always right.

–Markets distribute goods, services, and benefits rationally and efficiently.

–Market outcomes are inherently moral because they perfectly reflect talent and merit and so the rich deserve to be rich and the poor deserve to be poor.

–Any attempt to control market outcomes is inefficient and thus immoral.

–Any non-market activity is inherently suboptimal.

–If you *can* make money doing something not illegal, you *should* do it.

–As long as there is a willing buyer and seller, every transaction is moral.

–Any government solution, absent a total market failure, is a bad solution.

But, of course, markets properly understood are not actually efficient. So-called balances between supply and demand, while representing a fair approximation, do not in fact really exist. And because humans are not rational, calculating, and selfish, their behavior in market settings is inherently imperfect, unpredictable, and inefficient. Laypeople know this far better than experts.

Markets are a type of ecosystem that is complex, adaptive, and subject to the same evolutionary forces as nature. As in nature, evolution makes markets an unparalleled way of effectively solving human problems. But evolution is purpose-agnostic. If the market is oriented toward producing junk and calling it good GDP, market evolution will produce ever more marketable junk. *As complex adaptive systems, markets are not like machines at all but like gardens.* This means, then, that the following must be true:

–The market is often wrong.

–Markets distribute goods, services, and benefits in ways that often are irrational, semi-blind, and over-dependent on chance.

–Market outcomes are not necessarily moral—and are sometimes immoral—because they reflect a dynamic blend of earned merit and the very unearned compounding of early advantage or disadvantage.

–If well-tended, markets produce great results but if untended, they destroy themselves.

–Markets, like gardens, require constant seeding, feeding, and weeding by government and citizens.

–More, they require judgments about what kind of growth is beneficial. Just because dandelions, like hedge funds, grow easily and quickly, doesn't mean we should let them take over. Just because you can make money doing something doesn't mean it is good for the society.

–In a democracy we have not only the ability but also the essential obligation to shape markets—through moral choices and government action—to create outcomes good for our communities.

You might think that this shift in metaphors and models is merely academic. Consider the following. In 2010, after the worst of the financial crisis had subsided but still soon enough for recollections to be vivid and honest, a group of Western central bankers and economists got together to assess what went wrong. To one participant in the meeting, who was not a banker but had studied the nature of economies in great depth, one thing became strikingly, shockingly clear. Governments had failed to anticipate the scope and speed of the meltdown because their model of the economy was fantastically detached from reality.

For instance, the standard model used by many central banks and treasuries, called a dynamic stochastic general equilibrium model, did not include banks. Why? Because in a perfectly efficient market, banks are mere pass-throughs, invisibly shuffling money around. How many consumers did this model take into account in its assumptions about the economy? Millions? Hundreds of thousands? No, just one. One perfectly average or "representative" consumer operating perfectly rationally in the marketplace. Facing a crisis precipitated by the contagion of homeowner exuberance, fueled by the pathological recklessness of bond traders and bankers, abetted by inattentive government watchdogs, and leading to the deepest recession since the Great Depression, the Fed and other Western central banks found themselves fighting a crisis their models said could not happen.

This is an indictment not only of central bankers and

the economics profession; nor merely of the Republicans whose doctrine abetted such intellectual malpractice; it is also an indictment of the Democrats who, bearing responsibility for making government work, allowed such a dreamland view of the world to drive government action in the national economy. They did so because over the course of 20 years they too had become believers in the efficient market hypothesis. Where housing and banking were concerned, there arose a faith-based economy: faith in rational individuals, faith in ever-rising housing values, and faith that *you* would not be the one left standing when the music stopped.

We are not, to be emphatically clear, anti-market. In fact, we are avid capitalists. Markets have an overwhelming benefit to human societies, and that is their unmatched ability to solve human problems. A modern understanding of economies sees them as complex adaptive systems subject to evolutionary forces. Those forces enable competition for the ability to survive and succeed as a consequence of the degree to which problems for customers are solved. Understood thus, wealth in a society is simply the sum of the problems it has managed to solve for its citizens. Eric Beinhocker calls this "information." As Beinhocker notes, less developed "poor" societies have very few solutions available. Limited housing solutions. Limited medical solutions. Limited nutrition and recreation solutions. Limited information. Contrast this with a modern Western superstore with hundreds of thousands of SKUs, each representing a unique solution to a unique problem.

But markets are agnostic to what kind of problems they solve and for whom. Whether a market produces more solutions for human medical challenges or more solutions for human warfare—or whether it invents problems like bad breath for which more solutions are needed—*is wholly a consequence* of the construction of that market, and that construction will always be human made, either by accident or by design. Markets are meant to be servants, not masters.

As we write, the Chinese government is making massive, determined, strategic investments in their renewable energy industry. They've decided that it's better for the world's largest population and second-largest economy to be green than not—and they are shaping the market with that goal in mind. By doing so they both reduce global warming *and* secure economic advantage in the future. We are captive, meanwhile, to a market fundamentalism that calls into question the right of government to act at all—thus ceding strategic advantage to our most serious global rival and putting America in a position to be poorer, weaker, and dirtier down the road. Even if there hadn't been a housing collapse, the fact that our innovative energies were going into building homes we didn't need and then securitizing the mortgages for those homes says we are way off track.

Now, it might be noted that for decades, through administrations of both parties, our nation *did* have a massive strategic goal of promoting homeownership—and that what we got for all that goal-setting was a housing-led economic collapse. But setting a goal doesn't mean then going to sleep; it requires constant, vigilant involvement to see whether the goal is the right goal and whether the means of reaching the goal come at too great a cost. Homeownership is a sound goal. That doesn't mean homeownership by any means necessary is a sound policy. Pushing people into mortgages they couldn't truly afford and then opening a casino with those mortgages as the chips was not the only way to increase homeownership. What government failed to do during the housing boom was to *garden*—to weed out the speculative, the predatory, the fraudulent.

Conventional wisdom says that government shouldn't try to pick winners in the marketplace, and that such efforts are doomed to failure. Picking winners may be a fool's errand, but *choosing the game* we play is a strategic imperative. Gardeners don't make plants grow but they do create conditions where plants can thrive and they do make judgments about what should and shouldn't be in the garden. These concentration decisions, to invest in alternative energy or not, to invest in biosciences or not, to invest in computational and network infrastructure or not, are essential choices a nation must make.

This is not picking winners; it's *picking games.* Public sector leaders, with the counsel and cooperation of private sector experts, can and must choose a game to invest in and then let the evolutionary pressures of market competition determine who wins *within* that game. DARPA (the Defense Advanced Research Projects Agency), NIST (the National Institute of Standards and Technology), NIH (National Institutes of Health), and other effective government entities pick games. They issue grand challenges. They catalyze the formation of markets, and use public capital to leverage private capital. To refuse to make such game-level choices is to refuse to have a strategy, and is as dangerous in economic life as it would be in military operations. A nation can't "drift" to leadership. A strong public hand is needed to point the market's hidden hand in a particular direction.

Markets as Machines vs. Markets as Gardens

Understanding economics in this new way can revolutionize our approach and our politics. The shift from mechanistic models to complex ecological ones is not one of degree but of kind. It is the shift from a tradition that prizes fixity and predictability to a mindset that is premised on evolution. Compare two frames in capsule form:

Machine view: *Markets are efficient, thus sacrosanct*

Garden view: *Markets are effective, if well tended*

In the traditional view, markets are sacred because they are said to be the most efficient allocators of resources and wealth. Complexity science shows that markets are often quite inefficient—and that there is nothing sacred about today's man-made economic arrangements. But complexity science also shows that markets are the most effective force for producing innovation, the source of all wealth creation. The question, then, is how to deploy that force to benefit the greatest number.

Machine view: *Regulation destroys markets*

Garden view: *Markets need fertilizing and weeding, or else are destroyed*

Traditionalists say any government interference distorts the "natural" and efficient allocation that markets want to achieve. Complexity economists show that markets, like gardens, get overrun by weeds or exhaust their nutrients (education, infrastructure, etc.) if left alone, and then die—and that the only way for markets to deliver broad-based wealth is for government to tend them: enforcing rules that curb anti-social behavior, promote pro-social behavior, and thus keep markets functioning.

Machine view: *Income inequality reflects unequal effort and ability*

Garden view: *Inequality is what markets naturally create and compound, and requires correction*

Traditionalists assert, in essence, that income inequality is the result of the rich being smarter and harder working than the poor. This justifies government neglect in the face of inequality. The markets-as-garden view would not deny that smarts and diligence are unequally distributed. But in their view, income inequality has much more to do with the inexorable nature of complex adaptive systems like markets to result in self-reinforcing concentrations of advantage and disadvantage. This necessitates government action to counter the unfairness and counterproductive effects of concentration.

Machine view: *Wealth is created through competition and by the pursuit of narrow self-interest*

Garden view: *Wealth is created through trust and cooperation*

Where traditionalists put individual selfishness on a moral pedestal, complexity economists show that norms of unchecked selfishness kill the one thing that determines whether a society can generate (let alone fairly allocate) wealth and opportunity: trust. Trust creates cooperation, and cooperation is what creates win-win outcomes. High-trust networks thrive; low-trust ones fail. And when greed and self-interest are glorified above all, high-trust networks become low-trust. *See*: Afghanistan.

Machine view: *Wealth = individuals accumulating money*

Garden view: *Wealth = society creating solutions*

One of the simple and damning limitations of traditional economics is that it can't really explain how wealth gets generated. It simply assumes wealth. And it treats money as the sole measure of wealth. Complexity economics, by contrast, says that wealth is *solutions*: knowledge applied to solve problems. Wealth is created when new ideas—inventing a wheel, say, or curing cancer—emerge from a competitive, evolutionary environment. In the same way, the greatness of a garden comes not just in the sheer volume but also in the *diversity and usefulness* of the plants it contains.

In other words, money accumulation by the rich is not the same as wealth creation by a society. If we are serious about creating wealth, our focus should not be on taking care of the rich so that their money trickles down; it should be on making sure *everyone* has a fair chance—in education, health, social capital, access to financial capital—to create *new* information and ideas. Innovation arises from a fertile environment that allows individual genius to bloom and that amplifies individual genius, through cooperation, to benefit society. Extreme concentration

MARKETS: Machinebrain View

The rich deserve to be rich,
the poor deserve to be poor

Market economy outcomes
reflect the unequal distribution of
talent and effort and therefore
are moral and fair

Equality
implies tyranny

**Markets are
perfectly efficient**

People are rational,
calculating, and selfish

The pursuit of
self-interest is moral
because it leads to
the greater good

The market is always right
and is self-correcting

The only way to build
a prosperous society
is to harness people's
self-interest

Government
isn't the solution;
it's the problem

Market solutions are
always the best solutions

Government's attempts to
help people only hurt them

My money
is my money

Competition
=
wealth creation

Wealth is created
by "great men"

Unfettered markets
are meritocracies

Market outcomes
are fair by definition

The current
market arrangement
is the right arrangement

Markets self-correct
and should be allowed to

If you can make money at it,
it has to be OK

Government solutions
are bad, inefficient,
corrupt and distorting

Government spending
and programs are wasteful

MARKETS: *Gardenbrain View*

Market arrangements
are moral arrangements
if they are fair

My wealth is a
consequence of living
in my society

Equality of
opportunity creates true
competition and more
wealth for society

**Markets are effective
if well constructed**

People are emotional,
approximating, and reciprocal

Markets, like gardens,
must be tended

Markets, like gardens,
can be over-tended.
Too much weeding and tending
will result in no growth
or collapse

Markets, like gardens,
are man-made constructs
and must be tended in order
to work well

Helping every citizen
effectively compete is
the other central role of
government

The central role of
government is harnessing
the power of markets
in pro-social ways

Who is rich and who is
poor in a society is largely
determined by prior market
arrangements

Progressive taxation
is essential to maintaining
true competition

Market outcomes are
mostly a consequence of the
arrangement of market
forces; they are fair only if the
arrangement was fair

The rate of wealth
creation in a society increases
with the number of diverse
able competitors

Markets are
inherently unstable

Wealth is a consequence
of the creation of novel
solutions to society's problems

More solutions = more wealth

Markets, like gardens,
if left untended, will
become overrun with weeds
and will collapse

Unfettered markets,
like untended gardens,
always result in destructive
concentration of power
and wealth

Eliminating
anti-competitive
concentration of power
and wealth is a central role
of government

of wealth kills prosperity in precisely the same way that untended weeds overrun and then kill gardens.

Wealth creation is maximized *only* by maximizing the number of robust diverse competitors in the market. The more potentially "fit" players you can field, the more likely your team is to succeed. Equality of opportunity, then, isn't just a moral imperative. It's an economic imperative. Making sure everyone gets a fair shot isn't being nice; it's bowing to necessity. Unfortunately, the politics of the last three decades has led to a concentration of wealth without modern precedent that has undermined equality of opportunity and thus limited our overall economic potential.

Inequality and Economic Crisis

The election of Ronald Reagan in 1980, under the banner of "limited government" and "trickle-down economics," marked the start of a Thirty Years War against the middle class. Since then, the share of income the richest 1 percent earn has gone from 8.5 percent to 24 percent while the bottom 50 percent of Americans have seen their share drop from 18 percent to just 12.5 percent. If this trend continues, by 2040, the top 1 percent will garner 37 percent of the income and the bottom 50 percent just 6 percent of total income! At that point or well before it, our economy will have collapsed. In the meantime, we are at a level of wealth concentration not seen since just before the Depression, while tax rates on the top earners are at their lowest in decades.

What have been the costs of this imbalance? In November 2010, IMF economists Michael Kumhof and Romain Rancière published a seminal paper arguing that the economic crises of 2007–08 and 1929 were caused by the same phenomenon: radical income inequality.

In their paper, Kumhof and Rancière demonstrated that inequality and financial leverage create an unholy and fatal feedback loop. As the wealthy accumulate ever more money they generate price bubbles in real estate and other assets, which force all other participants in the economy to borrow more just to keep up. As the wealthy accumulate capital, their need to find return for these assets grows. The rich come to financialize their assets in the form of loans to—whom else?—the poor and middle class. Easy credit is the natural result of enormous pools of money seeking returns. As the poor and middle class borrow more in order to maintain lifestyles increasingly beyond their means, unsustainable leverage follows. In both 1929 and 2008, collapse was the inevitable consequence.

This crisis of income and wealth concentration is the most serious threat America faces today. The problem, to be clear, isn't inherently that the wealthiest among us make so much more than the poorest: inequality (of talent, effort, outcome) will always exist, and a wide spread from top to bottom is not necessarily malignant so long as there is a robust middle.

The problem is *concentration* and the hollowing out of the middle. Since 1980 an overwhelming proportion of the nation's wealth has concentrated at the very top. Today, the top 1 percent account for more wealth than the bottom 90 percent. That is not American. The middle has shrunk, the ranks of the poor have grown, and the United States now has the wealth distribution of a Third World nation. And whereas wages used to track productivity, they no longer do: American workers are ever more productive, but the wealthy are capturing those gains. Our aggregate national GDP may be higher today than it was in 1980, but when most of the additional wealth is in the hands of a few, most of us cannot be robust participants in the economy.

This is not just unfair; it's unhealthy. The researchers Richard Wilkinson and Kate Pickett, in their much-discussed book *The Spirit Level*, reveal that across the fifty states and then across nations as well, a pattern of correlation emerges so strongly as to assert causation: the higher the level of inequality, the higher the level of social pathology.

This is true of obesity, depression, violent crime, infant mortality, incarceration, pollution, and on and on. Concentration of wealth makes the entire society sick, and America is Exhibit A of this phenomenon.

This situation did not arise by accident. It is not something beyond our control, like today's weather. It is the direct and wholly predictable result of a 30-year experiment in trickle-down economics and market-fundamentalist politics—an experiment concocted by Republicans but never dismantled and often sustained by Democrats.

In this section, we identify the intellectual and political components of the right-wing economic theory of action, and aim to replace them with a new approach we call "middle-out economics."

Trickle-down Economics

Traditional economics, if taken literally, not only implies but necessitates market fundamentalism. If you believe the economy is a self-regulating machine, then you must believe that government intervention in the market is inherently bad.

The right's theory of action is thus to "limit" government. In management of the state, this translates into deregulation of business activity so that corporations, once unfettered, can lower costs, make more money, and (theoretically) create more jobs. In management of the economy, it means using tax policy to put more wealth in the hands of the wealthiest so that they can invest it in job-creating businesses. The Reaganites who pushed this agenda called it "supply-side economics," but it came to be known more enduringly as "trickle-down economics"— the idea being that money will trickle its way down from wealthy capitalists to everyday Americans.

That's the theory. Politically it has been a great success. The rhetoric of shrinking government and not punishing "job-creators" is dominant in American public life. The policies that support the rhetoric—personal income tax cuts for the wealthiest, cuts in capital gains taxes, cuts in the corporate income tax, rollbacks of the estate tax— have been left unchanged, plus or minus, by presidents of both parties since Reagan. The theory begat a political and policy consensus that even the Great Recession has barely nudged.

Unfortunately, there is one way trickle-down economic theory has failed: empirically. Average household income looks like it's 50 percent higher today than when Reagan took office—but that average is deceptive. Most of the gains in income during these three decades have gone straight to the top, particularly the top 1 percent. And the modest income gains of the middle between 2010 and 1980 look even less impressive when we consider that the average household now has more people working many more hours just to keep up. In practice, this has meant wage stagnation for the middle class, who've taken on ever more debt to keep up with the Joneses.

In their groundbreaking book on the policy choices behind inequality, *Winner-Take-All Politics*, Jacob Hacker and Paul Pierson meticulously explore the real dollar impact of rising inequality. One example sticks out: If the income distribution for all Americans had remained constant since 1980, the average American family would be earning $64,395, which is $12,295 and 24 percent more than they do today. If Americans had this much more to spend, and the nation this much more in its tax base, the economy would not be struggling as much as it is in 2011.

To understand why the low-wage, high-consumption, high-debt implementation of trickle-down economics has been such a failure—for everyone but the top 1 percent, that is—it's necessary to examine one of its core intellectual foundations: the notion that redistribution of wealth is inherently illegitimate and ineffective.

Redistribution, Spending, and Recirculation

This claim is sometimes offered up in cartoonish accusations of socialism. But in its more serious form, it is that redistribution kills the profit motive, is less efficient than market forces, and thus works to decrease overall wealth. By contrast, goes the claim, incentivizing those with capital to accumulate even more—even if it results in great and inherited inequality—is more consistent with American principles of liberty and free enterprise.

Let's take each piece of the claim in turn. To begin with, increases in income tax rates generally do not make already wealthy capitalists less likely to pursue profit or to engage in job-creating economic activity, whether starting a business or buying a car. It is absurd to claim that hedge fund managers would work less hard if the taxes they currently pay on carried interest were to increase from 15 percent to 50. In fact, a persuasive case could be made that a person who kept only 50 percent of his billion dollars in annual income, rather than 85 percent, would work close to 33 percent harder. Yes, there is a point of diminishing returns past which workers keep too little of the value their work creates, their incentive to work hard diminishes, and overall growth slows. We are nowhere near that. After the tax increases under the first President Bush and President Clinton, income tax rates were much higher than today—and yet this country enjoyed in the 1990s an unprecedented economic expansion and period of job creation. (And while we don't advocate the 90 percent marginal rate of the 1960s, we would note that America's growth rates were never higher than during that period of supposedly job-killing high taxes).

Next, the trickle-down economics crowd posits a false choice between government-mandated redistribution on the one hand and free markets on the other. But of course, this agenda—as exemplified by the Reagan rewrite of the tax code and the Bush perpetuation of it—is itself government-mandated redistribution of wealth: to the already wealthy. The "state of nature" does not dictate preferential treatment of capital over work, or regressivity of taxation, or the tax-free inheritance of unearned wealth and power: these are all consequences of man-made rules. The question, then, is not whether redistribution but in which direction.

Where we will agree, in small part, with trickle-down proponents is that the word "redistribution" is not an optimal word. Redistribution—whether uttered by its fans or foes—implies a one-time transaction, in which money is moved from point A to point B, where it then remains inert. That is clearly wrong.

But there is an even deeper misconception at work here. Conventional Machinebrain wisdom conceives of and

describes government activity as "spending." The following dictionary definition reveals why such a conception is
misleading and damaging:

> **spent** |spent|
> *past and past participle of* spend. *(adj.) having*
> *been used and unable to be used again: a spent*
> *matchstick.* • *having no power or energy left:*
> *the movement has become a spent force*

The association we have with the word spending is that
when government does it, *our money is gone.* The unconscious assumption is that our tax dollars are swept into
piles and burned or poured down a drain. The unconscious
assumption of course is rooted in a Machinebrain metaphor. The government, like a car engine, uses up money
like fuel. Of course, this ignores the fundamental reality of
the role of money in an economic ecosystem as essential
lifeblood that circulates throughout it again and again.

In this Gardenbrain sense, government does not *spend*
money; it *circulates* it. It does not *redistribute* money; it
recirculates it. Social Security is the largest line item of
government "spending" in the budget. But Social Security
is simply a collateralized savings account. Understood as
circulation, Social Security's main benefit isn't to keep the
elderly from living in cardboard boxes, although that is a
fine thing, but to ensure that they continue as dynamic
consumers in our economy. Social Security circulates

money back to the citizens who contributed to it in the first place, *and is then circulated again by them*, generating increased economic activity that allows others to be paid, to contribute to Social Security and then to receive those benefits in the future, in an endless and essential positive feedback loop that sustains and expands our economy. If Social Security truly were "spending," then our economy would be getting smaller and our nation's net worth would be shrinking as a consequence of its growth.

To varying degrees, all government economic activity is some form of circulation. Medicare is a system that allows retired workers to continue to participate in the economy by preventing them from being impoverished by medical costs. Military spending to a great degree circulates money back into the communities where our defense industry provides high-paying jobs. Even the lowly, lazy, useless bureaucrat is some small business's best customer.

Government doesn't spend money like it's a perishable or a consumable good. Government circulates money, and the flow, direction, and pace of that circulation are determined by policies our elected leaders choose. And this brings us to a pivotal point: for over three decades, as Hacker and Pierson detail in *Winner-Take-All Politics*, our leaders have chosen an economic program that chokes off circulation and allows a tiny minority to hoard blood.

The market, of course, is the prime circulator of wealth in

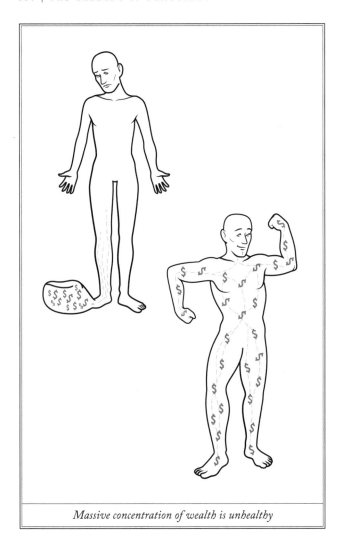

Massive concentration of wealth is unhealthy

an economy. But the public policies of this age of greed have created—by design—historic distortions in the private economy. Today the richest 1 percent of Americans has more wealth than the bottom 90 percent. The richest 1 percent collects twice as much annual income as the lower 50 percent. That is not circulation; it is clumping and clotting. When a single big toe is as big as a watermelon and contains twice as much blood as the entire head and torso—the body has fallen grotesquely out of balance. Left untreated, it will die. But when you have good circulation, the entire body grows stronger. Recirculation of wealth is as necessary to the economy as recirculation of blood is to the body, and that principle is at the heart of the program we propose.

Middle-out Economics

Our program is the antithesis of trickle-down theory. It's what we call middle-out economics, and its essence is simple: circulate wealth in ways that bring prosperity to the middle class so that it can buy goods and services and set in motion a feedback loop that benefits everyone—rich and poor—over the long term. Middle-out economics does not rely on the droppings of the super-rich. It starts with the broad middle to generate wealth and pushes that wealth outward so that it can circulate throughout the economy.

Trickle-down economics takes care of a few great men, on the mistaken idea that we can count on them to create jobs for the rest of us. Middle-out economics starts with the rest of us. It says that we are the engine of wealth creation. When the broad middle has the earning power to drive an economy, everybody is better off—including wealthy entrepreneurs who meet the demand of the middle. Even a hard-nosed industrialist like Henry Ford understood this when he paid his assembly line workers higher wages than the market said he needed to—not out of altruism but out of a long-term understanding that his employees were going to be his customers and needed to be able to afford a Model T.

Trickle-down economics means lower income taxes on the rich, lower capital gains taxes, lower estate taxes, lower regulation, and lower investment in public goods like education and infrastructure. It is about empowering the few on the theory that the many can derive second-order benefits. Its action is top-down.

Middle-out economics means investing aggressively in the middle class, more focus on education and infrastructure, higher wages, and strategic public-private investment in high-potential arenas coupled with strongly progressive taxation and aggressive estate taxation. It is about empowering the many so that the few can derive second-order benefits—and set in motion another cycle of prosperity. Its action is middle-out.

Trickle-down vs. Middle-out economics

Progressive taxation is one key here. It blunts the natural mathematical tendency of markets to concentrate into winner-take-all monopolies. It keeps the economy healthy by circulating resources back into the general economy and thus sets off cycles of ever-increasing prosperity, opportunity, and comparative advantage. Another key is a robust and adaptive labor union movement—willing to push management *and* decalcify itself—to help workers increase productivity and then share in the gains of that productivity. Unions are a vital counterweight to concentrated corporate power. But they can become protectionist in their own right, indulging in the kind of zero-sum thinking that makes any adaption seem like an unacceptable concession.

Middle-out economics is not about being anti-rich. It's about making everyone richer over the long haul. It returns to a simple idea that Gardenbrain economics teaches: we are all better off when we are all better off. No one benefits more in the long term from recirculation of wealth through taxes and government spending than the rich or those who wish to be rich. An economy where 300 million citizens are vibrant consumers is a high-growth, high-profit, high-multiple economy. For the wealthy to pay a bit more in taxes now for that kind of economy later is good business.

We state simply that excessive concentration always harms the whole. Blood should flow from the core outward, not from a swollen extremity to the rest of the body. To put it in economic terms, wealth should be generated by, from, and for the middle class in ways that intentionally benefit the broad middle and only incidentally (though inevitably) benefit the wealthy few.

There are five core principles that undergird middle-out economics:

Grow from the middle out. Our theory of action takes Ford's insight and amplifies it: foster a healthy middle-class customer base with purchasing power and everyone will get richer. Create a positive feedback loop of prosperity by investing in the middle class. Our theory also says that "government spending" is not a one-time dump of cash into a rat hole; whether it's Social Security or education, it's just good recirculation. This is the approach the United States applied in the first three decades after World War II, a period of prosperity unparalleled in how sustainable and broadly shared it was.

Maximize the number of able, diverse competitors. The point of the economy—particularly in a democracy—is not to enrich the few but to empower the many. For a nation to thrive and to win in a global economic competition, it needs to put as many players on the field as it can. As the complexity theorist Scott Page has argued in *The Difference*, "diversity trumps ability." That is, the ability of a society to solve its problems is more dependent on the diversity of approaches it takes than on the ability of a few individuals. Diversity is not only nice and inclusive; it is smart and effective. This means ensuring that *all* our children get a healthy start. It means enabling more of our people to get the education they need to be generators of new ideas and skillful contributors to innovation ecosystems. It means increasing access to capital for aspiring small businesspeople of limited means. It means shifting our asset policies so that incentives to save, which today are tilted toward the already affluent, can be used to give working Americans a leg up. America leaves far too much talent untapped. Bad schools, poor health, unsafe neighborhoods, the absence of job skill ladders—all these keep a great proportion of our human power inactive.

Break up opportunity monopolies. It is a fact of economic life that both advantage and disadvantage compound. What we end up with are opportunity monopolies dotting and clotting the economic landscape. When we tax what Teddy Roosevelt called the "swollen fortunes" of a tiny few—vast fortunes made possible by the investments in public goods by prior generations—and recirculate that wealth in public goods like schools and health care so that the middle and bottom can participate in the economy—we are doing something good for the many *and*, in the long run, for the few. Hoarding may feel like the rational thing for the rich, but it is against their true self-interest, which is found not in clotting but in circulation to the whole. Concentrations of poverty follow concentrations of wealth. This is why we need to return to progressive taxation and much higher marginal rates on high-income Americans—not to punish success but to create the conditions for more success for more people. It's why America needs an extensive class-based affirmative action program to ensure that there is true competition of talent. It's why there needs to be a massive rebalancing of our asset and tax incentive policies, which today are invisibly coring the middle class and directing $400 billion a year to the already affluent or wealthy. The richest 5 percent of Americans get more than half of all the benefits of the exemptions and deductions in the tax code. We must realign our asset and tax-expenditure policy so that loopholes and tax benefits work to benefit the not-rich rather than further fatten the already rich. It is why we need to invest the revenues from these first two steps into research and development and incentives for the formation of businesses that create jobs in America—not for the illusory products of our metastasizing financial sector.

Promote true competition. In American policy today, we don't help people become rich; we reward the already rich for being rich. When you look at it closely, the ersatz capitalism of Wall Street and market fundamentalists is actually quite protectionist. The ideology of "free enterprise," as preached by anti-tax and anti-regulation activists, is used to prevent change to the current arrangement of economic power: don't regulate my company, don't touch my money, don't let more people in on the game I've rigged. Socialize losses, privatize profits. It's about defending capitalists; not capital*ism*. Such a defense of the current distribution of wealth might be tolerable if the status quo allowed for every American to compete purely on the basis of talent and merit. Do you really think it does? True capitalism is about making sure everyone is on the playing field, not just those who can afford the equipment. It is about upending the order of things continuously, not defending it. True capitalism is more competitive because it's more fair, and more fair because it's more competitive.

Harness market forces to national goals. Economic right-wingers insist that heroic individuals "do it themselves" and that such people are "self-made." This claim does not hold up under any serious scrutiny. Ford could not have created an auto industry without the roads necessary for them to travel on. He did not build those roads, let alone mark or map them. Amazon and Google did not create the Internet; the federal government did. No company in America has provided the infrastructure that made its lines of businesses possible, much less educated its own workforce. The question is not whether to have government in the economy but how wisely to deploy it. Government's job, in collaboration with the private sector, is to set great goals. The market's job is to unleash a truly competitive frenzy in pursuit of those goals.

We're All Better Off When We Are All Better Off

Limited-government advocates say they don't trust the government to spend your money. We say why trust the super-rich to spend your money? We say why not trust the people of the middle class to spend their own money? Like the trickle-down economics crew, we believe there is a goose that lays a golden egg in our economy. They think the goose is the top 1 percent. We think it's the broad middle class. *They think we're all better off when the rich are better off. We think we're all better off when we are all better off.*

We believe that nurturing an economy from the middle out and the bottom up is how this country can achieve and sustain real—earned, and unborrowed—prosperity of the kind that trickle-down has never once delivered.

To be sure: government needs to be smarter and more efficient in its role as circulator and investor. And there is no question that the animal spirits of capitalism and markets remain an unsurpassed force for innovation and solutions. We are pro-capitalism. In fact, we are fiercely so. What that requires is remembering what capitalism is supposed to be about—generating the most widespread competition possible so that society gets the most fruitful results possible.

Some may claim that we are calling for totalitarian leveling, for equality of outcomes. Absolutely not. A certain amount of inequality is inevitable and even beneficial. But we simply point out that too much inequality is as fatal to society as enforced equality. The distribution curve should look more like a bell than a hockey stick, with a big sweet spot of prosperity and security—as it was in the 1950s and 1960s. Unfortunately, since the 1980s, we have had the hockey stick.

The choice facing the United States is simple. Free-lunch trickle-down economics sounds great but is a proven loser. Grown-up middle-driven economics sounds harder but will get us back on track as a country. We can have an economy with only a few winners, or an economy where everyone who works hard wins.

Imagine two gardeners with plots of land side by side. The first rakes the seed so that it's spread more evenly; the second lets it be. When the seeds begin to sprout weeks later, the first gardener has fruit and vegetables all across her plot; the second has plants where the seed had clumped but otherwise barren land.

The moral is clear, and urgent for our times: When seed is spread unevenly, the garden yields less fruit. When it's spread more evenly, it yields more fruit. And this in turn yields more seed for the next season, which enables the evenly spread plot to yield still more fruit. In societies that have true prosperity, the rich don't get richer; *everyone gets richer.* America used to understand a simple, and very self-interested precept that benefited the entire country: *we are all better off when we are all better off.*

Of course, in societies with true prosperity, the government tends the garden of economic life. It seeds, it feeds, it weeds. The reframing of what an economy is and how it works necessarily changes the story of what government is and how it must work. That is the focus of the next section of the book.

V. Self-Government

Big What, Small How

What is government for?—The failure of "limited-government" ideology and the hollowness of its libertarian core—The inability of traditional progressive approaches to meet current challenges—A new conception of government as gardener—A new approach to how government should work

What is government for?

Over the last several years, this has been the dominant question of American politics. Yet so few leaders have offered coherent answers.

The Tea Party has energized the right in recent years but has offered little more than a reprise of unworkable ideas and worn rhetoric about "limited government." The left, meanwhile, has been in a defensive crouch, reluctant either to embrace Great Society methods of governing or to acknowledge their shortcomings. President Obama has offered up defenses of government in speeches. But defending government is not enough. There is a higher threshold, for the President and all of us: to articulate, during this time of flux, an affirmative theory of government.

What should we expect government to do? How should government be doing it? And when we say "government," just whom do we mean?

The current dissatisfaction with government is not a mere perception or marketing problem, as too many on the left still believe. It is a product problem. Government has for too many people become unresponsive, dehumanizing, and inefficient. And it has not successfully met the most serious challenges of our time. Only when we improve government itself will our satisfaction with it improve. Unfortunately, the American discourse on government has long been frozen in two dimensions: more vs. less government, big vs. small. We argue for an orthogonal approach: more government when it comes to setting great goals and investing to achieve them; less government when it comes to how we collectively meet those goals.

We call this theory of action "Big What, Small How." Our view is that it strikes the right balance of both strategic purpose and adaptive, competitive implementation. Big What, Small How is rooted in Gardenbrain. In the following pages, we dissect the Machinebrain approaches that dominate our politics: conservative (Small What, Small How); libertarian (No What, No How); and liberal (Big What, Big How). We show why they are lacking and then outline our new approach.

The Limits of Limited Government: Small What, Small How

Let's start by unpacking of the theory of "limited government," propagated most often by the right but too often unchallenged by the left. It holds that:

—Democratic government derives legitimacy from the people (yes);

—It should be limited and as close to the people as possible (all right);

—Its charge is to safeguard individual rights and liberties (okay, though how best to do that is a matter of contention);

—In so doing the government's scope of power is limited to a military to secure the territory, police to enforce laws, courts to adjudicate disputes, and some taxes to cover these costs (now comes trouble);

—Any other role for government is illegitimate, and any additional taxes constitute theft and push us toward communism (the nexus to reality loosens); and

—In any event, such redistributive policies are always inefficient compared to a free market (now that nexus is gone entirely).

This philosophy, if we can call it that, fails on three levels: theoretical, empirical, and political.

Theoretical emptiness. The right idealizes "free enterprise." But the way they invoke it presupposes a vacuum, the utter absence of context. It assumes that all people are equally free to learn or get capital or make beneficial connections and be "enterprising"—and that only evil government stands in the way of such freedom—when in fact, in the actual world, there is no such even spread of opportunity. "Free enterprise" assumes there is such a thing as an individual separate from the community, when in fact, an individual's ability to pursue life, liberty, and property—to live up to his or her full potential— is realized *only* in community. Markets themselves exist only as social institutions, with rules made by people not by nature or deities. Personal responsibility is vital but grossly insufficient. The context of opportunity defines so much of our ability to act—our true freedom.

Conservatives believe the less government there is, the more freedom, wealth, and happiness, and they point to miserable, impoverished totalitarian states as reverse proof of their belief. This is a shockingly simpleminded understanding of how freedom works. The right thinks that if you have a freedom axis and a government axis, the relationship between the two variables is inverse and yields a straight-line graph. We believe, based simply on having opened our eyes, that the graph in fact yields a bell curve.

That is to say, there is a sweet spot where more government *enhances* freedom. Indeed, increasing freedom is the job of government. Sometimes that means letting people do what they want. Often it means getting them to do what they don't want to, like paying taxes or not polluting, so that over the long term everyone can do more. The FAA prevents pilots from flying wherever they want but that increases our general freedom to fly. The SEC requires companies to truthfully state their results, which builds trust and enables us to buy stock as represented and without fear of fraud.

We agree that the sweet spot does devolve into a tail in which totalizing government stifles freedom, creativity, motivation, etc. But just because it's possible to over-manage a company, over-coach a team, or over-tend a garden doesn't mean that not managing, not coaching, and not tending makes sense.

Empirical failure. One obvious reason for the right's zero-sum, straight-line view of the relationship between government and freedom is the utter and unquestionable failure of communism as a method for organizing societies. But it doesn't follow that every step government takes is a step towards communism or serfdom. In fact, there is not a stable, prosperous democratic society on earth without activist government, extensive regulation, and high, progressive taxation. The history and unrivalled success of Western capitalist democracies is the story of more activist government.

Market fundamentalists would have us believe that our success comes *in spite* of government. There is literally no evidence for this. Indeed, as Peter Lindert writes in his comprehensive international study *Growing Public*, increased public investments have always resulted in increased economic growth, and the net costs of social spending are essentially zero. Common sense suggests why. If less were always better, then the least regulated economies would be the most successful economies. The opposite holds. It is, in fact, the rules, regulations, standards, and accountability that government provides that fuel and lubricate markets. It is the investment in schooling, infrastructure, and health that maximizes the number and capacity of participants in the private sector. A robust state is not mutually exclusive with a free market; it is required for it. This is why there is no robust private sector on earth that isn't accompanied by an equally robust public sector.

Consider that many of the 195 countries in the world have been running experiments in "limited government." All are abject failures. If minimalist government worked, Somalia would be rich, stable, and secure and Canada would be a hellhole. Afghanistan would be a coveted destination and Denmark would be like a leper colony. In the comfort of a think tank in a country with air-conditioning and running water, to say nothing of the rule of law, it is very easy for American right-wing libertarians to pontificate about slashing government to the bone.

But ask any of them where they'd move their families if they had to leave the United States. Few would choose Afghanistan—a limited government state if there ever was one—over, say, Sweden or Japan.

Now, one might contend that setting up this slippery slope to Somalia is as much a debater's cop-out as crying communism. Granted. But we state the case this way to highlight a simple truth: freedom isn't free. This is true not only in the sense that it costs blood and treasure to defend freedom. It is true also in the sense that freedom, in anything other than an academic conception—that is, in the real world, with other people—means limiting one's own sphere of action in the short term so that over the long term we can all do more.

Political failure. Perhaps the most practical test of the limited-government idea is whether its adherents, when they are in power, can put the idea into practice. They cannot. They never have. Ronald Reagan, who told us government was the problem and not the solution, increased government spending 69 percent during his administration and removed the stigma from massive budget deficits. George W. Bush gave us Medicare Part D, the Department of Homeland Security, and two wars that have cost trillions. We grant that there are many libertarian conservatives who, because of this political fact, are as frustrated with establishment Republicans as with Democrats. But libertarian conservatives have always had the luxury of criticism from the sidelines. They have never had to govern—until, perhaps, now.

Libertarian Blindness: No What, No How

It's worth pausing and addressing the heart of the limited-government view and its libertarian roots. Libertarianism is Machinebrain thinking at its worst. It rests on a linear understanding of social and economic systems and on the falsehood that humans are reliably and inherently rational, calculating, and selfish.

David Boaz, vice president of the libertarian Cato Institute, writes that "Libertarianism is the view that each person has the right to live his life in any way he chooses so long as he respects the equal rights of others." And that "Libertarians defend each person's right to life, liberty, and property—rights that people have naturally, before governments are created."

Unobjectionable, this may seem. Until you think about it. For this worldview assumes that *all* humans can be counted on to be rational and to *actually and always* defend every other person's rights. It also assumes that human societies are equilibrium systems, not prone to toppling over as a consequence of the actions of some of the participants. That is to say, it assumes that bad actors, those who do not respect other's rights, can exist in isolation, and that their behavior will not affect the behavior of everyone else.

Modern systems thinking shows these assumptions to be false. Humans are not rational and calculating and only some are cooperative enough to respect other people's rights. A significant part of any human population does not respect the rights of others and will act affirmatively, absent regulation, to subjugate others' rights to their own. Moreover, the behavior of these selfish non-cooperators influences others and pushes them to a tipping point of wholesale distrust. As a result, in societies where there are few curbs on or consequences for bad behavior, cooperation collapses and soon so does the society.

This is why any societies that are *truly* libertarian are in various states of civil war, and why the most cooperative societies with activist governments are the only prosperous, stable, and secure societies on earth. Libertarianism is a luxury available only in communitarian societies. If it were anything more, then somewhere there would be a high-functioning libertarian society.

In the prevailing narrative of political economy—told by Democrats as well as Republicans—regulation destroys prosperity by limiting the ability of businesses to operate and create value. That this is hogwash becomes obvious if we allow ourselves to see the evidence around us. Seatbelt laws didn't reduce the size of the auto industry; they increased it, as the safety and thus the marketability of driving increased. Food safety laws didn't decrease the size of the food business; they increased it, as consumers came to trust mass providers of food.

Despite claims to the contrary, we see with our eyes that the more highly regulated countries are the more prosperous ones and that countries with little or no regulation are more impoverished. Does this mean regulation is intrinsically good, or that more is always better? No. The former Soviet Union is a case in point. And even in non-outlier cases like India, the burdens of complying with regulation can inhibit growth. But as a general matter, regulation is essential for prosperity in just the way that tending a garden is essential for its productivity.

The libertarian thesis of limited government depends, again, on a 19th-century notion that an economy or a society is a closed system, like a gas-powered car engine. If you take away gas, the car will go more slowly or less far. The system has decreasing returns. There is a zero-sum relationship between its elements. On such a story of an economy, it follows naturally that if there is more government regulation, there must be less business activity. If taxation increases, then economic growth must decrease.

In fact, our economy isn't closed. It is open. The feedback loops aren't negative. They are positive. The elements of the system are not in zero-sum relationship to one another. They are in symbiosis.

Zero-sum economic reasoning suffers from what we call the plants-and-animals fallacy. In nature, it would be folly to assert that the way to create more animals would be to limit plants. Plants nourish animals, which spread the seed and increase the number of plants that can now sustain a greater number of animals. Ecologically, more of one thing doesn't mean less of another; in fact, it almost always means more. Relationships are not zero-sum; they are positive-sum. If you want more animals, you need more plants.

Limiting government to increase business makes no more sense than limiting plants to increase animals. Robust private enterprise requires robust state involvement and investment. This is not to say that big government is by definition effective government. In a non-equilibrium economy, the role of government is to eliminate harmful kinds of increasing returns, like speculation bubbles, and to encourage and propel pro-social kinds like the Internet revolution and the attendant wealth creation. Government can do this effectively or ineffectively; but it must do it.

Prosperity, after all, is a consequence of our ability to innovate. Innovation requires ever-increasing amounts of technology. That technology, in turn, can only be created and managed by people with ever-increasing amounts of training and education. The number of hours of schooling it takes to train someone to plow a field is orders of magnitude smaller than to train them to write computer code. Prosperity also requires more trade. More trade requires more infrastructure—not just roads and bridges, or airports and train stations, but also treaties, trade agreements, contracts, and the people who create them.

These investments don't just enable prosperity, they propel it. And the story isn't just that government does this once and then gets out of the way; it is about continually investing to sustain positive feedback. Limited-government theory is anti-growth and anti-prosperity. It refuses to acknowledge the way these collective investments propel innovation, and must be continually renewed.

The Failure of the Left: Big What, Big How

Ah, but the left doesn't fare much better. Though we think the left gets more things right than the right, it needs a wake-up call.

We have from progressives an approach to government that for decades has been on autopilot. At the center of this Obama has put forth some positive reforms that seek to re-imagine progressive governance, from Race to the Top in education to health-care innovation incubators to clean-energy challenge grants. But he has not made such initiatives the signature of his governing philosophy. More to the point, he has yet to spell out a governing philosophy, a big story of what government is for. For all the self-doubt and handwringing among progressives today, the reality is that we still live in a nation where the New Deal/Great Society template is dominant. Far too many of us accept a substantial state role in every aspect of society.

It turns out that the left is as prone as the right to the assumption that humans calculate their self-interest rationally. Where the left differs is in its penchant for top-down prescriptive solutions. This is a big what *and* a big how. This is progressive Machinebrain thinking. As James Scott describes in *Seeing Like a State*, his illuminating survey of social engineering schemes of the 20th century, the very idea of "social engineering" treats complex human problems as orderly, predictable, manageable. The trouble, of course, is that they are not. This desire to "bracket uncertainty," as Scott writes, is self-defeating in three ways: sclerosis, impracticality, and crowding out.

Sclerosis. In a society as dynamic as ours, problems come too fast, and big institutions are too slow. Bigness—whether at GM, AIG, or HUD—is maladaptive and creates great vulnerability and risk. Bigness means too much complexity of organization, and "complexity catastrophes"—the seizing up of systems too densely packed with networks—are beginning to become the order of the day in public life. In juvenile justice or public education or health care, real people pay the price for bigness and complexity catastrophes. Once upon a time in all these realms, someone built, on an industrial model and metaphor, a machine for solving a problem of that moment. And then people stopped running or adjusting the machine. Worse, sometimes they have locked the machine in place so that it cannot change. For instance, while unions are important and have surely improved the lives of millions of Americans, they have also left us with protectionist workplace rules that can undermine the adaptability of both public and private organizations.

Impracticality. What makes big government non-adaptive is not only its size and slowness. It is also its substitution of central expertise for on-the-ground practical knowledge. If this sounds like a classic right-wing talking point, well, so be it. It is truth. The reality is that when not only goals but also means are determined at the center, government is always a step behind reality. What real people end up doing is making end-runs and work-arounds—in the best case. In the worst case, as in the famines that followed collectivization in Soviet Russia, people are forced to live and die by the mechanistic rules. When instead the means are determined by those who can make close observation of the actual environment, and make sense of the patterns they perceive—again, whether in child welfare or hospice care—what becomes salient is practical, informal, intuitive, local knowledge. James Scott uses the Greek term *mētis*. You could call it common sense, know-how, the art of *doing* in a particular case: shepherding a particular patient to health, putting out a particular kind of house fire. The more top-down a state becomes, the less *mētis* it allows for.

Crowding out citizens. Another negative consequence of the big-government bargain is that we've stopped noticing all the ways that state action crowds out community and citizen ownership of problems and solutions. When Americans come to think of government as a vending machine—drop in the coins and expect a great society to come out—then good citizenship shrivels. Citizens start to think their role is to pay, consume, and kick the machine when they're unsatisfied. Government, as it has developed, too often drains first the incentive and then the capacity of groups of people to address problems on a human scale. Economist and Nobel laureate Elinor Ostrom has written powerfully about groups of citizens, all around the world, who have created their own networks to allocate resources, police a commons, punish free riders, and sustain high norms of mutual obligation and strong reciprocity. These networks certainly collaborate with government but they did not emerge from it. One needn't be Newt Gingrich to ask why progressives can't foster more such nongovernmental networks. Progressives say "it takes a village," but then too often rely on an agency. We acknowledge that some problems—like the interstate behavior of rapacious health-insurance firms—happen on a scale that requires action of equal reach. We insist, however, that many more problems happen on a scale that we citizens can and should own and address.

The Government We Need: Big What, Small How

Our call, in short, is for an end to the big vs. small government debate and for the beginning of *government that is big on the what and small on the how*: a stronger hand in setting great national goals and purposes; a lighter touch in how we reach those goals. Government, as we explain below, should be less a service provider and more a tool creator; less wielder of stick than of carrot; less the parent than the coach; and less the vending machine than the toolkit for civic action. A Big What, Small How government should set the bar high and invest fully in a great springboard—then let people, through dedication and practice, compete to get over the bar.

This approach recognizes that both strategic direction *and* adaptability are essential to any successful endeavor: strategy, so that the energies of the nation can be focused; adaptability, so that quick response to changing local conditions can influence the direction. This is the pattern of biological evolution: central nervous systems whose most sensitive receptors to change are at the edges.

To be very clear, we are not calling for a Reagan-style devolution that pushes responsibility down without providing the resources to do the job. We are not calling for unfunded mandates. We are calling for *funded* mandates

Theories of Government

Left	Right	New
Big government	No/limited government	Self-government
Services & programs	Do-it-yourself	Tools
Mom	Dad	Coach
Mandates	Silence	Goals
Rules	No rules	Incentives
Centralized	Decentralized	Polycentric
Big what / big how	Small what / small how	Big what / small how

and, even better, funded challenges. If government is to set bigger whats, it must invest accordingly. When we say citizens should be doing more of the how, we mean they should get the tools to do it. The idea that states (or communities) should be laboratories for democracy is meaningful only if the labs are funded sufficiently to run good experiments.

Many libertarians will resist the "Big What" side of our equation, warning of the unintended consequences that will ensue when the government sets broad goals and direction for private sector activity. But unintended consequences are the very font of innovation—not least in the private sector. Whether welcome or unwelcome, they are what give rise to new technologies and force competitors to adapt. Unintended consequences are precisely why the other side of our equation is "small how." We can't know whether a push for clean energy might one day lead to a revolution in early learning, any more than we might have predicted that the space race would have given us Teflon-coated skillets.

Limited-government advocates say that the state should do precious little because every act creates unintended consequences. But unintended consequences cannot be used as an excuse for inaction because inaction has its own unintended consequences, no less potentially harmful than the kind that result from action.

From the other side, some strong statist liberals will ask why we are being so timid. Why not federalize and centralize more activity? They will point to Social Security and say, here is an example of something government-run that works great—let's do more. We agree, actually, that a program like Social Security that involves an implied promise of benefits, straight income transfers, and the cutting of checks is best administered centrally by the state. There are certain activities where the economies of scale, the stability of need, or the cleanness of execution lend themselves well to execution by the government. Our point is that the list of such activities is not long and is getting shorter every day. Where the behavior of people and the emergence of trends are dynamic and continuously affect the nature of the endeavor, government needs to be more nimble, more adaptive, more responsive, and thus far less involved directly in the delivery of service.

We believe, as did FDR, in "bold, persistent experimentation" in government. But today we do not (fortunately) have a world war to distort the experiments. So we have to be far more disciplined in our experimenter's mindset: We have to be ambitious in our goals, imaginative in our means, ruthless in our evaluations, and aggressive in funding successes and starving failures.

The Elements of a "Big What"

Let's explore in greater depth, then, the elements of a *big what* for government:

To **set strategic goals** for the community, whether it's a nation, state, or city, and to do so with an implicit moral opinion that some outcomes are preferable to others. Clean energy is better than dirty. Going to college is better than not. Real food is better than junk food. Generating credit for productive economic activity is better than casino capitalism. When a market is left to itself, what ensues is an anti-social race to the bottom. The government's job is to forge broad agreement on goals and set in motion pro-social races to the top.

To **equip every citizen** with the greatest possible capacity —and equal opportunity—to join in the pursuit of those goals. This begins with common defense and police and courts and so forth. It means spending some of the common wealth—generated by taxes—to improve education and health and to ensure that the disparities between the wealthiest and the poorest never grow so wide that it undermines social mobility. It also means investing heavily where it's strategic and where national scale is essential, whether that's physical or technological infrastructure, and where only the government can build a wealth-generating commons that market participants alone would never venture to build.

To **generate trust** and to encourage cooperation. In a capitalist society, competition is not actually the prime imperative—cooperation is. Trust is the most precious form of capital, generating prosperity and security. That is especially so in a society like ours, so prone to fragmentation along so many lines. One of government's core purposes is thus the active promotion of trust and creation of social capital—not just a personal ethic of honesty but a collective condition of reciprocity generated by shared experiences. This is why national service matters, and why it should be mandatory: it enables people who wouldn't otherwise cross paths, let alone work together, to do so. It's why any government-funded project should require robust collaboration as a condition of funding. It's why, at a local level, seed funding that helps neighborhood groups get started is a wise investment.

To **sustain *true* competition** and break up concentrations of wealth and power that are unearned and self-perpetuating. In a non-linear, critical-complexity world like ours, advantage and disadvantage compound rapidly. Inequities of opportunity become self-reinforcing. This entails redistribution of wealth, yes, through progressive taxation. But let's be very clear. Conservative leaders already rule in such a way as to redistribute wealth—toward the already wealthy. This is not consistent with any idea of America. Market fundamentalists contend that inequality is natural and inevitable. We concede that talent is not equally distributed and outcomes will never be equal. But in true capitalism there is true competition, in which unearned and inherited advantage is leveled so that talent can compete against talent.

Elements of an Effective "Small How"

If government is to do more what and less how, here are some of the ways to approach the *how*:

Radically re-localize. If, as we propose, the federal government is to forge national goals, then it needs also to radically re-localize the means—and, in contrast to the "devolution" of the Reagan era, actually provide robust funding for those local means and intentionally link up all the local experiments. Obama's Race to the Top education initiative is a good example of combining leverage at a higher level of government in an area of strategic national interest with responsibility and creativity at lower levels. We would go even further. There should be strong national content standards in education, with far more federal education funding. And that funding should then go to a diverse ecosystem of educators who develop a multitude of ways to get kids to the standard. Thus, the parents of each public school should take far more ownership of the quality of the education within the building. That means having more choice about how to staff and run the school, and on what style of pedagogy, but it also means taking more responsibility for the results. Creating high and common standards. Funding them. Pushing authority ever downward. Setting off waves of experimentation. And then forming national, even global, networks to allow the local experiments to learn from one another. In nature, as ecologist Rafe Sagarin has observed, systems that sense change are always decentralized so that threat detection is as local as possible—but then all those local sensors are always connected into networks so that response can be coordinated for the whole. The same approach—creating local laboratories, generating bottom-up innovation, connecting innovators across geographies—should be applied to homeland security, as Sagarin has suggested, to energy policy, health care, economic development, and other arenas. To flip the old creed: think locally, act globally.

Be the citizen's hardware store. As government relocalizes authority and responsibility, it must also provide the resources to enable locals to act robustly and to be networked with one another. By resources we do not mean only cash; we mean tools to empower citizens to solve problems on their own: apps that enable citizens and even cities to share information and solutions without middlemen; rewards for leaders who take on the responsibility of organizing Dunbar groups; templates and guides to enable Dunbar groups—aka small groups of citizens—to plant gardens, clean up streets, create business districts; and requirements that government agencies like public libraries be civic connectors and incubators for such activity. In this age of social entrepreneurialism, we also want government to incubate the next Teach for America and the next City Year so that civic innovators can experiment and take successful experiments to scale.

This is a vision that the technology guru Tim O'Reilly has described simply: "government as a platform." Government should create open standards and systems, and encourage the flowering of citizen-created, data-driven apps. He means this both literally and figuratively, and we agree. Our default settings should shift. Government, wherever possible, should be the catalyst for crowd-sourced citizen action and when necessary, a provider of resources and expertise. Think about a dilapidated city block, with boarded-up buildings, litter, and graffiti. Rather than wait for the municipal government to fix it up, what if neighbors—using tools (both digital and physical) and some funding from the city—organized to fix it up themselves?

Be a smarter prime contractor. Liberals too often see government as a service provider of first resort. That outlook is inadequate to the times. Government bureaucracies are generally incapable of providing high-quality, low-cost services that adapt to the changing requirements of citizens. At every level, we think the imperative should be to shift responsibility for executing what are now government services to private competitive organizations. This can and should include non-profits, particularly where profit motives in the delivery of social services would be harmful. Government must become a highly disciplined contracting agent with the ability to set standards, create transparency, and hold accountable those who do the work. Wherever possible it should get out of lines of business that it can't do better than others. Government printing offices are a relic. The licensing of drivers or hunters or boaters should be franchised. As with any franchise model, there'll be uniform standards of product and service and branding—but local owners of the actual organization will deliver the service.

It's true that there's plenty of contracting already happening in government, particularly at the municipal level, and that this privatization has often yielded waste and subpar performance. Too much government contracting today merely replicates the non-adaptive, non-competitive dynamics of government agencies. We are calling on government, like an effective foundation or venture investor, to get far better at running competitions. It has to develop more competence to assess performance, replicate successes, and fire failures. It has to challenge the firms in its operating ecosystem to learn from each other, to improve and exchange practices, to pool resources and leverage learning.

Create and amplify positive feedback loops. One of the central features of open complex systems like our economy is feedback loops, both good and bad. Government plays a central role in setting both kinds in motion. Governing to anticipate socially destructive feedback loops like financial bubbles or storms of fraud is a central role. But a modern government should seek also to create hurricane-like storms of pro-social activity as well. The national government can and should create prosperity and positive feedback loops by using its capacity to birth new markets through basic research (as DARPA Net begat Google) and to create demand through its enormous buying power and leverage (as should be happening in alternative energy).

Offer pounds and pounds of prevention. An effective epidemiologist invests more in prevention than in cure, nipping epidemics in the bud rather than trying to contain them after the fact. Every part of government needs to think more like a public health officer: to be mindful always of desired outcomes, track closely trends in behavior, look at the world like a network of networks, identify the key nodes of virulence, and focus energy and effort on those nodes to foster contagions of good and to contain contagions of bad. To put it simply, focus on prevention rather than cure. In the last 20 years, urban policing has moved this way, as shown by the emergence of national coalitions of cops and children's advocates like Fight Crime, Invest in Kids. So now must efforts to combat obesity or teen pregnancy or to promote stable families or responsible environmental behavior. Government is in a unique, bird's-eye position to map the network and set off the epidemics it wants. It can and should make networked collaboration and early intervention—things that most public entities are not incentivized today to pursue— actual conditions for continued public funding. Government should scale up proven, evidence-based pilots that show that investment early in the pipeline yields far more dividends than investment at the end. Does that mean that starting today, the state should stop funding prisons and fund only early learning? Of course not. It does mean, though, that the state today must set an intention and a timeline, at the end of which we are indeed investing far more in early learning than in prisons.

Design more nudges. By this point it should be clear that we believe government should not be neutral—in fact, it should be very clear and vocal—about pro-social goals and activities. More even than Cass Sunstein, the head of President Obama's Office of Information and Regulatory Affairs and co-author of *Nudge: Improving Decisions About Health, Wealth, and Happiness*, we believe that such judgment should sometimes be expressed in direct government action. But like Sunstein, we are fans of what he describes as "nudging": designing "choice architectures" that give citizens the liberty to choose but steers them toward the more pro-social choices. Whether it's designing opt-outs rather than opt-ins for retirement saving, or labeling food ingredients or household energy use, nudging and the application of behavioral science to policy-making is smart and adaptive.

Tax more strategically—and progressively. America's tax code today is an incoherent jumble. The power to tax should be used more strategically, in line with the broad goals the national government sets. We should use the tax code like a personal trainer: to get us in shape by reinforcing good habits and punishing bad ones. A strong carbon tax, to reduce energy consumption. Soda and candy taxes, to attack obesity. Estate taxes, to correct for unearned advantage and to stave off aristocracy. But the most strategic tax of all is more progressive income taxation, with fewer loopholes, for both individuals and corporations. Allowing the accumulation of uncoordinated tax breaks to release a corporation like GE from paying any taxes whatever is profoundly irresponsible. Skewing our helter-skelter system of tax incentives for housing and education toward the affluent, such that the wealthiest Americans receive more than $95,000 in tax benefits while middle-income families receive a few hundred dollars and poor families actually face penalties for saving, is counter to any theory of opportunity. Letting over a third of the nation's wealth "clot" among just 1 percent of our people—as we will do if the next 30 years are like the last 30—is national suicide. Progressive taxation is the only way for a society to create the virtuous circle of ever-increasing shared prosperity.

Create incentives and rewards for over-performance. Ex-ante regulation and ex-post punishment are the two tools that government uses most often to affect the behavior of firms and individuals. A third tool is missing, the critical one from an adaptive government perspective: incentives for excellence. Government anticipates and punishes underperformance. It also must create massive and system-wide incentives for over-performance. There should be more competitions to design better systems across government—in building codes, early learning, health care, car gas mileage. There should be challenge awards like the X Prize—a prize given by a private foundation to innovators in the field of manned spacecraft—in every part of government. The strategic recognition and rewarding of over-performance is the fastest way to set off cascades of innovation in the public sector. In the case of pollution, bad performers should pay extra fines that subsidize rewards for high performers. Over-performers should get "EZ Pass" advantages—expedited regulatory approval, easier access to credit for productive investment, and more—so that government can help the excellent perpetuate their success and pressure the bad to end their failure.

Weed relentlessly. Evidence-based practice (and funding) sounds obvious but isn't routinely practiced (or funded). It must be the actual method of government. When the experimentation we champion has yielded successful models—in, say, the delivery of primary care—they should be replicated. When the evidence says a program has failed or outlived its usefulness, it should end. And government should be looking continuously to end things—indeed, it should have a goal of ending a percentage of programs every year—so that those resources can be deployed, in an adaptive way, to new challenges. The Obama Administration has quietly and powerfully made evidence-based funding—and de-funding—a more common way of doing business in the federal government, in arenas like education research and health innovation. We want more. The point, as in our entire philosophy, is not to end government, but to end the way we do government. Government should be living, organic, evolving—not inert, inanimate, and unchanging.

Reclaiming Democracy

We note, however, that before this kind of repurposing can happen, the rules of democratic practice and governance must first change. There is one underlying issue that all Americans, whatever their politics, most confront: the creeping corruption of a campaign finance system that treats money as speech, pushes politicians to spend time courting the moneyed, enables lobbyists to become unelected lawmakers, and gives credence to the rising belief in America that our government is bought and paid for. The more the appearance and reality of such corruption reinforce one another, the more challenging it becomes to earn the buy-in of the public in *any* reimagining of government's role. This is why at least in part, we applaud the citizen activism of the Tea Party: here is a group of Americans who, however misguided their view of policy and muddied their motives may be, want to reclaim ownership of government and regain the attention of our elected leaders.

This is why we as citizens—left, right, and all points otherwise—must first push through an agenda to decalcify the processes by which government in America operates:

–Reform redistricting. Modern-day gerrymandering has made districts more ideologically homogenous and our politics more polarized. Congressional districts should be drawn independently of the parties, and optimized for a mix of voter viewpoints rather than incumbent protection.

–Restrict money in politics. Most Americans think politics is a game rigged by those with money. They are right. The *Citizens United* ruling by the Supreme Court to remove restraints on corporate spending in elections is egregious, but it only underscores a long-standing truth about campaign finance in America: plenty of activity that is legal is still corrupt. It's time for dramatic restrictions on campaign finance.

–Stop the revolving door. It is a measure of how far our national ethics have drifted when members of Congress and senior executive staff leave their jobs to work for the corporations they once regulated— and no one cares. This too is a sin of both parties and it must end.

—Reform the filibuster. The rules of the U.S. Senate, as we have seen in recent years under both Republican and Democratic control, are designed *against* adaptability. The filibuster has made the Congress essentially a supermajority-only body on most hard issues. That must end.

—Reinvigorate voting. Voting in the United States should be mandatory, so that representation of the people is a reality and not a fiction. Efforts to suppress voter turnout among voters of color and youth, fueled mainly by Republicans, are shameful and should be shamed out of existence.

These kinds of reforms are not the wish list of naïve do-gooders. They are the necessary remedies for a body politic that has succumbed to what Mancur Olson called "the logic of collective action": a sclerotic accretion of narrowly focused interest group demands that lock up the state's ability to move or change. Reforming the rules of governance maximizes the speed of public response to public challenges. It pushes out polarization, engages all the people, and encourages problem-solving. It redesigns government for adaptability, making it more clear-eyed in setting strategy and more nimble in executing it.

Adapt or Die

Of course, in the meantime, there is great opportunity to shift the country's understanding of what government is for. Our theory of government cannot be put in a box. It's not left or right or in-between. It's "conservative" in that it values local practical knowledge and it wants to put markets and competition to good use to radically increase adaptability and accountability. It's "liberal" in that it proposes a strong meliorist role for the national government to set ambitious goals, level the playing field, equip everyone to compete fairly and fully, and identify great failures of the commons that need to be addressed by shared action. It's about national identity *and* local power. It's about networked localism. Most of all, it's about effectiveness.

The Big What, Small How approach to governing ourselves is not an excuse to slash public spending. It is not a call for a bossier nanny state. It is, quite simply, a framework for *owning* government in every sense: taking title to it and taking responsibility for it. Big What, Small How is just how a savvy gardener operates. A gardener does not make the vine climb or the rose bloom. But he does decide whether it will be vegetables or flowers. He does plant accordingly. He does distinguish between good growth and bad, between a wanted tomato and an unwanted weed. Most of all, he knows that if he doesn't do the work in the garden, no one else will.

When John Adams was a young man, his father died, leaving him title to property in Braintree, Massachusetts. Adams learned that he had inherited not only a house but also a set of duties. The elders of Braintree informed Adams that he was now responsible for managing roads and other public works and in particular was now charged with the building of a much-needed bridge. Adams protested that he knew nothing of bridge construction. The elders told him, in essence, *Figure it out.* And Adams did, hiring the experts and supervising them on behalf of the town. Our theory of government, like our theory of citizenship, expects each of us to be more like young John Adams: more responsible than we had ever realized for figuring it out.

Government is what a society creates to solve common problems that each of us alone could not solve. We agree with the right that the job of government is to maximize individual opportunity. We just believe that the way to do that is to maximize the trust, cooperation, and equal opportunity that frames up each individual's starting prospects. We agree with the left that the job of government is to ensure fairness and justice. We just believe that the way to do that is to put more responsibility on people to govern themselves by using more local, less distant, and more responsive means.

By binding us together to pursue broad national ends and

equipping us to develop our own means, our Big What, Small How approach can fundamentally reorient how most Americans see government: not as them, but as *us*. We are government. We own it—if, to echo Franklin, we can keep it.

Will our new theory of government, if implemented, create new problems? Of course. It will create its own unintended consequences and its own patterns of turf, faction, and short-termism. It will force new trade-offs. But it addresses the underlying problems of our politics today, and it does so by making government fundamentally more adaptive and accountable than it is today. A practice of continuous and cold-eyed *evolution* can replace the passionate rhetoric of perpetual but never requited *revolution*.

It is not enough, as we said at the outset, to defend government reflexively—or even thoughtfully. It is not enough to triangulate or buy time by cherry-picking a few ideas from anti-government activists. It is time, rather, for all of us to engage in sincerity the debate that the right opened in cynicism. It is time to set in motion a repurposing and a rebalancing of the roles that state and citizen play in the quest for true liberty and enduring justice. Big What, Small How represents our best opportunity for an adaptive form of progressive self-government. It is time to put it into practice.

VI. Harvest

We Reap What We Sow

*Review of the argument—Democracy's gardens—
The true meaning of liberty—The test of
pragmatism—The freedom of responsibility,
and vice versa*

IN OUR LAST BOOK, *The True Patriot*, we made a moral argument that in order for freedom to be meaningful, actionable, and equitable across a society, free individuals must curb their appetites, limit their hoarding, and share both bounty and sacrifice: in every sense of the word, *govern* themselves.

In these pages, we have been making the practical analogue to that moral argument, fueled by the latest teachings of science and the oldest lessons of experience.

Our view is framed by the need to move from a 19th-century Machinebrain to a 21st-century Gardenbrain. Only if we replace the obsolete and limiting metaphors of yesterday can we hope to meet the challenges of today and tomorrow.

We began with self-interest, that propulsive force of human activity, and described a new narrative in which **true self-interest is mutual interest.** That is not just our personal view; it is the view afforded by a second scientific Enlightenment that shows us to be strongly reciprocal, networked, and interdependent instead of purely selfish, atomized, and independent. We laid out, upon this foundation of enlightened self-interest, a new conception of citizenship that takes into account the contagious nature of all behavior and the responsibility in a democratic republic that each of us bears to act as if *society becomes how you behave*—because it *does*.

From there, we considered the price we have paid for imagining the economy to be a machine, always self-correcting to equilibrium, rather than a garden, always blooming in forms that can be glorious or cancerous. The power of this metaphor shift—from machine to garden—is best appreciated in its necessary empirical consequences. In a complex adaptive system like a garden or a market economy, it turns out that we cannot let others wither while we blossom, for in the end their blight is ours and so *we are all better off if we are all better off*.

Finally, we asked what this all means for the role of government. A complex adaptive systems worldview—a vision of the world as contingent, connected, and continually in flux—reveals the folly of both Machinebrain centralized bureaucratic government and the libertarian fantasy of limited government. What we need now, more than ever, is not big or small government but government that is *big on the what and small on the how*: government that sees the world as networks, systems, and cascading contagions and operates to harness what it can, toward a shared notion of the common good—and get out of the way of what it cannot. It should focus more on what to grow and less on how to grow it.

Throughout, we have understood and depicted our democracy as an array of gardens. The garden of our civic and community life. The garden of our markets and economy. The garden of our government, from local to national. In every variation, the theme is simple. We are more connected than we know. We and our systems follow the laws not of the clockmaker but of the gardener. Our imperatives are not to let things be once they are set in motion but rather to *tend*. The gardener understands the dynamics of the natural systems around him and has the humility to know he does not *make* nature. But he understands equally that it is his active hand that *shapes* it; that separates the garden from the wild.

We have been depicting, in short, a grown-up version of freedom. What does freedom mean? Only children and other immature people truly believe that it means only "I get to do whatever I want." Only the immature believe that a slogan like "Don't tread on me" makes any restriction tyrannical. Adults know that limiting some of our own freedom on the margins enables us—is the *only* thing that enables us—to enjoy more and better freedom at the core. No high-functioning family, sports club, business, or country governs itself by letting people just do what they want. No high-functioning person governs himself that way either. Cooperation more than autonomy makes winners. We give up taxes, time, and license. We get the security, infrastructure, and rules that enable success. Freedom isn't free. It costs a little freedom.

Freedom is also what enables each of us and all of us to adapt, to evolve: to make progress. History teaches us that great civilizations usually succumb to sclerosis, paralysis, and decay in the face of change. American civilization has a built-in advantage, which is that we are adaptive by design. But nothing is foreordained. If we remain wedded to fixed ideologies that ignore our pressing needs, all of our American can-do spirit will be for naught. If we push for a politics of independent thinking, we may yet find a way to fulfill America's promise. It's entirely our choice. We reap what we sow.

Well into the 21st century now—long past our battles against tyrannical kings, many generations since the closing of our frontier, a century since new forms of industrial capitalism concentrated power and wealth in ways that diminished our civic equality—Americans would do well to remember that teamwork is what we need for this diverse nation to be greater than the sum of its individual parts.

This is not just our wish and our ideal. We are, in making

this case, being relentlessly pragmatic—not pragmatism as cynical calculation but pragmatism as a method of assessing *what works*. This is another great American tradition: rejecting ideology for ideology's sake and remembering always that the value of a value is simply whether it leads to good outcomes for the society. Values are not opinions; they are, in essence, facts. That is, they have consequences. The actual, empirical consequences of libertarian selfishness and atomization are disaster. The ultimate measure of a value system should be *Does it work for us*? We have tried to show in these pages that as a matter of scientific theory and real experience, libertarian ideas of market, citizenship, and state do not work any better than statist, command-and-control ideas.

So God bless the American individual. And God bless the American team that enables the individual to thrive. We do not accept a false choice between individual rights and collective responsibility. We say you can have both. You can't have either *unless* you have both. And to win, you *must* have both. With inalienable rights come inalienable responsibilities.

There is a notion—embodied today by the Tea Partiers—that the real meaning of the Revolution was that all government is tyranny, that collective action is collectivism and therefore oppressive. But the reality of the Revolution and of the intellectual, moral, and political atmosphere that yielded it is that our nation's founders were formed by a philosophy of freedom as mutual obligation—of *rights as duties*. Thomas Jefferson understood, when he wrote the Declaration, that to be free means to be bound to others, that to look out for oneself means attending to others. The entire colonial experience—to say nothing of the interregnum between independence and ratification—teaches us one thing: When it's every man (or state) for himself, no one stays free for very long. Freedom is just another word for *we're all in it together*. If it is to mean anything, freedom must mean responsibility. In the end, freedom *is* responsibility.

As Jefferson and his cohort passed from the scene, the second generation of United States citizens—leaders like Daniel Webster—came to the fore. They had been infants during the Revolution and thus were its first true inheritors. They had to sustain the republican ideals of their ancestors at a time when a grand chase for wealth had begun to define national purpose. Though we may idolize the Founders and Framers, it is to Webster's generation that every American since has had the closest relation. It falls to us, as it fell to them, to decide: with independence long achieved, can we now do the daily work of interdependence? Can we mature, as a people, and claim *freedom to* as much as *freedom from*? Can we make democracy work? Can we adapt to the great challenges of our time or will we fail?

We are all second generation Americans. Great seeds have been sown for us. Let us now tend, with wisdom and humility, the gardens of our democracy.

ACKNOWLEDGMENTS

OUR AIM IN THIS BOOK was to extend the arguments being made across the sciences about the deep nature of systems and people to the civic sphere. It's our strong belief that these new insights will ultimately radically reshape politics, economics, and our theory of government.

As such, if we've made a contribution at all, it is one of synthesis and interpretation, not original scholarship. Without the scholarship and research of many other people, this book would have been impossible.

No one was more influential in this regard than our friend Eric Beinhocker, author of *The Origin of Wealth*. Eric's work was essential to our thinking. His patience with our questions and his shaping of our manuscript were above and beyond the call of duty.

We were deeply influenced by conversations with many other scholars. Jenna Bednar, Francis Fukuyama, Jon Haidt, Mike Lind, Jeff Madrick, Scott Page, Rafe Sagarin, and Michael Sandel made us see things in new ways. We may not have followed their counsel fully but we always benefited from it greatly.

Our friends in the world of politics and ideas were also enormously helpful. Rob Stein has been a great mentor to us both. He and Jabe Blumenthal, Bob Borosage, Bill Budinger, Jon Cowan, Alan Durning, Ed Lazowska, Tara McGuinness, Jen Palmieri, Andy Rich, Jeremy Rosner, and Michael Tomasky sharpened our thinking and were all wonderfully critical of our early drafts.

Our amazing designer Deborah Brown not only shaped the look and feel of this book but also suggested its title! Our flexible and adept publisher at Sasquatch Books, Gary Luke, made publication a breeze. Both were our partners in *The True Patriot*, which preceded this book, and we're grateful the partnership continues.

Finally, to Leslie Hanauer and Jena Cane, and to our children, we give deepest appreciation for putting up with our constant antics with great patience and love.

READING LIST

IF YOU'RE INTERESTED in exploring the ideas in this book more deeply, here are some of the books that influenced our thinking a great deal. Please also visit our website: GardensofDemocracy.com.

The Age of the Unthinkable: Why the New World Disorder Constantly Surprises Us and What We Can Do About It, Joshua Cooper Ramo (Back Bay Books, 2010)

Big Citizenship: How Pragmatic Idealism Can Bring Out the Best in America, Alan Khazei (PublicAffairs, 2010)

Born to Be Good: The Science of a Meaningful Life, Dacher Keltner (W. W. Norton & Company, 2009)

The Case for Big Government, Jeff Madrick (Princeton University Press, 2010)

Chaos: Making a New Science, James Gleick (Penguin, 2008)

Common as Air: Revolution, Art, and Ownership, Lewis Hyde (Farrar, Straus and Giroux, 2010)

Complex Adaptive Systems: An Introduction to Computational Models of Social Life, John H. Miller and Scott E. Page (Princeton University Press, 2007)

Connected: The Surprising Power of Our Social Networks and How They Shape Our Lives—How Your Friends' Friends' Friends Affect Everything You Feel, Think, and Do, Nicholas A. Christakis and James H. Fowler (Back Bay Books, 2011)

Deep Economy: The Wealth of Communities and the Durable Future, Bill McKibben (St. Martin's Griffin, 2008)

Deep Simplicity: Bringing Order to Chaos and Complexity, John Gribbin (Random House, 2005)

Democracy's Discontent: America in Search of a Public Philosophy, Michael J. Sandel (Belknap Press of Harvard University Press, 1998)

Diversity and Complexity, Scott E. Page (Princeton University Press, 2010)

Governing the Commons: The Evolution of Institutions for Collective Action, Elinor Ostrom (Cambridge University Press, 1990)

Growing Public: Volume 1, The Story: Social Spending and Economic Growth Since the Eighteenth Century, Peter H. Lindert (Cambridge University Press, 2004)

How Markets Fail: The Logic of Economic Calamities, John Cassidy (Picador, 2010)

Inventing America: Jefferson's Declaration of Independence, Garry Wills (Mariner Books, 2002)

Liberty and Freedom: A Visual History of America's Founding Ideas (America: A Cultural History), David Hackett Fischer (Oxford University Press, USA, 2004)

Linked: How Everything Is Connected to Everything Else and What It Means, Albert-László Barabási (Plume, 2003)

The Logic of Collective Action: Public Goods and the Theory of Groups, Mancur Olson (Harvard University Press, 1971)

Moral Sentiments and Material Interests: The Foundations of Cooperation in Economic Life, Herbert Gintis, Samuel Bowles, Robert Boyd, and Ernst Fehr, editors (The MIT Press, 2006)

The Nature of Technology: What It Is and How It Evolves, W. Brian Arthur (Free Press, 2009)

Nudge: Improving Decisions About Health, Wealth, and Happiness, Richard H. Thaler and Cass R. Sunstein (Penguin, 2009)

The Origin of Wealth: Evolution, Complexity, and the Radical Remaking of Economics, Eric D. Beinhocker (Harvard Business School Press, 2006)

The Origins of Political Order: From Prehuman Times to the French Revolution, Francis Fukuyama (Farrar, Straus and Giroux, 2011)

The Real Wealth of Nations: Creating a Caring Economics, Riane Tennenhaus Eisler (Berrett-Koehler Publishers, 2008)

Reclaiming Conservatism: How a Great American Political Movement Got Lost—And How It Can Find Its Way Back, Mickey Edwards (Oxford University Press, 2008)

Seeing Like a State: How Certain Schemes to Improve the Human Condition Have Failed, James C. Scott (Yale University Press, 1999)

Self-Rule: A Cultural History of American Democracy, Robert H. Wiebe (University Of Chicago Press, 1996)

The Social Animal: The Hidden Sources of Love, Character, and Achievement, David Brooks (Random House, 2011)

The Spirit Level: Why Greater Equality Makes Societies Stronger, Kate Pickett and Richard Wilkinson (Bloomsbury Press, 2011)

The Theory Of Moral Sentiments, Adam Smith (Kessinger Publishing, 2004, originally published in 1759)

Trust: The Social Virtues and The Creation of Prosperity, Francis Fukuyama (Free Press, 1996)

Up from Conservatism, Michael Lind (Free Press, 1997)

ABOUT THE AUTHORS

ERIC LIU is an author and educator based in Seattle. He served as a speechwriter and a senior domestic policy adviser to President Bill Clinton.

NICK HANAUER is a Seattle-based entrepreneur and venture capitalist. He is active in many progressive civic and philanthropic organizations and causes.

In 2007, Liu and Hanauer co-authored *The True Patriot*.

N O T E S

NOTES

NOTES

NOTES

NOTES

NOTES

NOTES

NOTES